FROM SUNSPOTS TO STRAWBERRIES...

TO STRAWBERRIES...

Answers to Questions

Answers to Questions

Also available:
From Beetroot to Buddhism...
From Comets to Cocaine...
From Crystals to Crocodiles...
From Elephants to Einstein...
From Limestone to Lucifer...
From Mammoths to Mediums...

FROM SUNSPOTS TO STRAWBERRIES...

Answers to Questions

RUDOLF STEINER

Fourteen discussions with workers at the Goetheanum in Dornach between 30 June and 24 September 1924

RUDOLF STEINER PRESS
LONDON

Translation revised by Matthew Barton

Rudolf Steiner Press
Hillside House, The Square
Forest Row, East Sussex
RH18 5ES

www.rudolfsteinerpress.com

Published by Rudolf Steiner Press 2002
Previous English edition translated by Gladys Hahn and published
under the title *The Evolution of the Earth and Man and the Influence of the
Stars* by Anthroposophic Press and Rudolf Steiner Press 1987

Originally published in German under the title *Die Schöpfung der Welt und
des Menschen Erdenleben und Sternenwirken* (volume 354 in the *Rudolf
Steiner Gesamtausgabe* or Collected Works) by Rudolf Steiner Verlag,
Dornach. This authorized translation is based on the 3rd edition, edited
by Paul Gerhard Bellman, and is published by kind permission of the
Rudolf Steiner Nachlassverwaltung, Dornach. Drawings in the text are
by Leonore Uhlig and are based on Rudolf Steiner's original blackboard
drawings

A catalogue record for this book is available from the British Library

ISBN 1 85584 112 6

Cover by Andrew Morgan Design
Typeset by DP Photosetting, Aylesbury, Bucks.
Printed and bound in Great Britain by Cromwell Press Limited,
Trowbridge, Wilts.

Contents

Main Contents of the Discussions

1 *Discussion of 30 June 1924*
Creation of the world and man—Saturn, Sun and Moon stages of Earth evolution

The whole earth once lived and thought—and was all possible things; and not until it became a corpse was it able to create the human being. Unthinking concepts of the earth's creation out of a dead, spiralling, primal fog. What a substance looks like is dependent only on the degree of warmth or heat within it; heat or fire is the original element underlying everything. In the Saturn phase of earth evolution there were as yet no solid bodies, nor any air, but only heat. The first thing that occurred in this cosmic essence of heat was a cooling process. What happens when something in which nothing apart from heat could previously be distinguished starts to cool down? Air arises. In the Sun stage of Earth evolution air is the first thing to arise—a warm airy mist. First (in the Saturn stage) man was present; and subsequently (at the Sun stage) the animals appeared, formed from what could not become man. The animals are related to the human being but they came about later. When heat cools down still further, then not only air forms but also water (that is the Moon stage of Earth evolution); and from water plants shoot up, for they originally grew not on the earth but in water. Our present birds are the descendants of the original animals, which developed at the Sun stage. The life of the human embryo in the womb is similar to life on the Old Moon; the woman's period is a memory of the Old Sun state. Fertilization on the Old Moon was a kind of cosmic fertilization. Our present earth stage, the fourth stage of evolution, gives rise to solid earth and mineral substance through a further cooling process. How the mineral element is quite differently integrated in the human being and birds. The errors of Darwinism. Fish as birds taken up by the water; they did not arise until the Old Moon period. Fever as memory of the Saturn stage.

2   *Discussion of 3 July 1924*
  ## Creation of the earth—origin of the human being
  In its former states the earth was a kind of living being. The water of the ancient Moon period was a thick fluid in which were dissolved all substances that are nowadays solid, and the air was a thick mist containing mainly metals and sulphur. It would have seemed like being in a world egg. Not until the moon's departure during the earth stage did the earth die, thus acquiring the mineral realm, which is dead. But only as a result of this did conditions allow plants, today's animals and the human being to arise in their present form. The effect of silicic acid contained in the air on the human senses, nerves and hair. Silicic acid or silica is an enormously beneficial remedy. How all conditions changed for animals and human beings after the moon left the earth. Once the moon worked on us from without, external fertilization could occur.

3   *Discussion of 7 July 1924*
  ## What anthroposophy and science have to say about earth strata and fossils
  The present earth has a solid core of 70 to 80 substances, and around it is the atmosphere with oxygen and nitrogen. There are always also other substances contained in the air, but only in very small quantities. These include carbon, hydrogen and sulphur. Geology estimates the age of geological strata on the basis of the fossils found in them, but also has to consider strata-inversions and reconfigurations. In the Alps everything that was built up in layers was later thrown about and intermingled. The origin of fossils and casts of animals. The present form of the earth shows us that it was alive at a time when human beings and higher animals did not yet live. The human being could only awaken to consciousness once the earth had gradually died away. We evolve out of the dead earth. Today we breathe in oxygen and breathe out carbon dioxide, while the plants breathe in carbon dioxide and breathe out oxygen. Just as today's plants build themselves up through carbon, so earlier plants nourished themselves from nitrogen. Today we exhale a compound of carbon and oxygen while formerly we exhaled a compound of carbon and nitrogen—the terribly poisonous prussic or hydrocyanic acid. In the same way that the earth once had prussic acid, so now the comets have it. Where the sun and the stars are is empty space, a vacuum that would

immediately suck you up and shatter you. Stars are hollow, empty
spaces.

become coarse in contrast. Most animals have a very large taste-brain, of which there are only small vestiges in the human being. But he has the capacity to form ideas with his transformed taste-brain. What makes the human being more perfect than other creatures and why he is nowadays so clumsy. By turning their attention to spiritual science human beings will become more adroit again.

10   *Discussion of 9 September 1924*
The planetary influences on animals, plants and rocks
The planets will one day all reunite with the earth and become one body with it. The planets do not have the same solidity as the earth; description of physical conditions on Mars. Years of grub and May-bug profusion and their connection with the four-year Mars-rhythm. The sun exerts its major influence on everything on earth that is dead and must be reawoken to life each year, while the moon only exerts an influence on living things. Mars only influences what lives in finer realms, in feelings; and the other planets influence soul and spirit. The present conditions on Mars are the same as they were on earth at an earlier stage of evolution, and today's Jupiter represents a future condition of the earth. The plants gain their scents from the planets and their colours from sun and moon. The sun takes a whole cosmic year to give colours to a stone. Mountain and alpine herbs have greater healing effect than lowland plants. Wild strawberries thrive especially where there are rocks containing a small amount of iron. The rose is an oil-gatherer; it finds in garden cultivation a great deal of what there is little of in the wild. It is enormously important for agriculture to know about soil.

11   *Discussion of 13 September 1924*
The weather and its causes
The appearance of sunspots and their connection with the weather. Sunspots arose millennia ago; they multiply and will continue to multiply until, in the far future, the sun is eventually extinguished altogether. The ice age will recur in five, six, seven thousand years; it will not occur exactly in the same region of the earth as it once did. Such interruptions to the smooth course of evolution derive from the fact that the surface of the earth continually rises and falls. The origin of air and ocean currents, and also electro-magnetic currents, and their influence on weather conditions. The dispute

between Fechner and Scheiden about the moon's influence on the weather. The repetition of the same moon position after 18 or 19 years. Venus' transit of the sun every hundred years. The hundred-year calendar. The weather is enormously influenced by forces which arise in the atmosphere itself. Lightning does not arise through electricity but as a result of the air discarding its own heat. Human brains have become much more rigid in recent centuries than they were previously.

12   *Discussion of 18 September 1924*
Form and origin of the earth and the moon — causes of volcanic activity
How does zigzag lightning arise? The earth's form is actually a tetrahedron that has grown spherical, and most volcanic mountains lie along its edges. The volcanoes that lie along the sides of the tetrahedron are the original fire-spewing mountains; other volcanoes arose later. The Falb calendar or almanac with predictions of 'critical days' of weather, earthquakes, volcanic eruptions etc. in relation to the constellations. Cosmic warmth raying into the earth. The origin of the moon. Julius Robert von Mayer's reply to the question: How can it be that the sun gives us so much warmth but does not grow cold? The sun is a space that sucks in, continually sucks comet mass towards it. It sucks in fine etheric formations in the universe, which are almost spiritual, and nourishes itself from these etheric masses, these comet masses.

13   *Discussion of 20 September 1924*
What is the aim of anthroposophy? Biela's comet
The way people react to anything new. The strangest examples of how new scientific discoveries and inventions are received. The harmful effect of eating potatoes. Eating potatoes has in recent centuries greatly contributed to a general decline in health. Spiritual science researches the spirit in a scientific way. The comet that was expected in Paris in 1773 and that was thought to bring the end of the world; its subsequent appearances in 1832, 1845/46, 1852 and 1872. Littrov's text on the 1832 comet (Biela's comet) and on comets in general. The expected comet does not appear as a comet at all, in fact, but comes as a fine shower of meteorites; it gave itself as nourishment to the earth, and, because it is a medicine, a cosmic medicine, relieves nervousness in human beings. Nothing will ever

be solved in the social realm until science once more becomes spiritual. Only through spiritual knowledge do we learn to understand social conditions. Marxism depends on an erroneous science. The workers' question will assume a quite different form when people view everything from a spiritual perspective.

14   *Discussion of 24 September 1924*
Where do we come from? Earth life and star wisdom

Why the workers' question, the social question has become such a burning issue. In the way the social question is addressed, spiritual knowledge is lacking. Originally people had an extensive knowledge of the stars, but nowadays all they know of the stars are calculations; and they are unable to respond to what is spiritual in the stars. The stars all have an influence on human spiritual and cultural life. From the moon come the forces of all reproduction on earth, from the sun come the forces of growth and from Saturn the forces of thinking. Since people do nothing but calculate they have forgotten the real human being, and treat him like a cog in a machine. All agricultural produce has been declining in quality for decades throughout the world. Something is always destroyed in the brain when people think. The whole body — with small exceptions such as the skeleton etc. — is completely renewed in seven or eight years. The body we have in the first seven or eight years of our life comes from our mother and father; but this is cast off completely and after seven or eight years we have a new body that we ourselves must build up. The active force that later builds up the body comes from the world of spirit. We do not only live by virtue of what we eat but also from finely dispersed nutrients in the air, which we inhale. The food we get by eating is used, for example, to continually renew our head, while the nutrients we need to acquire fingernails for instance, come to us from the air. Through the food we eat we take up the physical, but we take up soul and live with it through respiration. The human being lives the same number of days as he breathes in a day: 25,920 breaths. If we regard a human life as one cosmic day, we arrive at the cosmic year: $72 \times 360 = 25,920$ years.

Publisher's Foreword

The truly remarkable lectures — or, more accurately, question and answer sessions — contained in this book, form part of a series (published in eight volumes in the original German)* dating from August 1922 to September 1924. This series features talks given to people involved in various kinds of building work on Rudolf Steiner's architectural masterpieces, the first and second Goetheanums in Dornach, Switzerland. (The destruction by fire of the first Goetheanum necessitated the building of a replacement.) A vivid description of the different types of workers present, as well as the context and atmosphere of these talks, is given by a witness in the Appendix to the first volume of this English series, *From Elephants to Einstein* (1998).

The sessions arose out of explanatory tours of the Goetheanum which one of Steiner's pupils, Dr Roman Boos, had offered. When this came to an end, and the workers still wished to know more about the 'temple' they were involved with and the philosophy behind it, Dr Steiner agreed to take part in question and answer sessions himself. These took place during the working day, after the mid-morning break. Apart from the workmen, only a few other people were present: those working in the building office, and some of Steiner's closest colleagues. The subject-matter of the talks was chosen by the workers at the encouragement of Rudolf Steiner, who took their questions and usually gave immediate answers.

---

*347–54 in the collected works of Rudolf Steiner, published by Rudolf Steiner Verlag, Dornach, Switzerland. For information on English translations, see the list on page xvii.

After Rudolf Steiner's death, some of the lectures — on the subject of bees — were published. However, as Marie Steiner writes in her original Preface to the German edition: 'Gradually more and more people felt a wish to study these lectures.' It was therefore decided to publish them in full. However, Marie Steiner's words about the nature of the lectures remain relevant to the present publication:

> They had, however, been intended for a particular group of people and Rudolf Steiner spoke off the cuff, in accord with the given situation and the mood of the workmen at the time. There was no intention to publish at the time. But the very way in which he spoke had a freshness and directness that one would not wish to destroy, for this would take away the special atmosphere that arose in the souls of those who asked the questions and him who gave the answers. It would be a pity to take away the special colour of it by pedantically rearranging the sentences. We are therefore taking the risk of leaving them as far as possible untouched. Perhaps it will not always be in the accustomed literary style, but on the other hand it has directness and vitality.

In this spirit, the translator has been asked also to preserve as much of the original style, or flavour, as possible. This might necessitate that readers study a passage several times, trying to bring to mind the live situation in which the talks were given, before the whole can be fully appreciated.

S G

Rudolf Steiner's Lectures to Workers at the Goetheanum

GA (*Gesamtausgabe*) number

Creation of the world and Man — Saturn, Sun and Moon stages of Earth evolution

Rudolf Steiner: Good morning, gentlemen! Has anyone thought of a question?

Herr Dollinger: I would like to ask if Dr Steiner would speak again about the creation of the world and the human being. There are many newcomers here who have not yet heard it.

Rudolf Steiner: Could I speak again about the creation of the world and of humanity, since many new workers are here? I will do this by first describing the original conditions on the earth, which have led on the one hand to all that we see around us and on the other hand to the human being.

Now man is really a very, very complicated being. If people think they will be able to understand him by dissecting a human corpse, they are mistaken, for naturally they will not arrive at a real understanding. Just as little can they understand the world around us if all they do is collect stones and plants and examine them separately. We must take account of the fact that what we examine does not show at first sight what it actually is.

You see, if we look at a corpse, perhaps soon after the person has died — he still has the same form, if perhaps a little paler — we can see that death has seized him, but he still has the same form that he had when alive. But now think: how does this corpse eventually look if we do not cremate it but let it decay? It is destroyed; there is no longer anything at work in it that could build it up again; it disintegrates.

People often have a chuckle when they read the beginning of the Bible, and they are right to do so if they understand it to say that once upon a time some god formed a man out of a clod of earth. People regard that as impossible and naturally they are right. No god can come along and make a human being out of a lump of earth; it would be no more a man than a statue is, however similar the form might be — no more than the mud-man or snowman children make can actually walk. So people are right to smile at the idea of some divine being making the human being from a lump of earth.

That corpse that we were looking at is in fact, after a certain time, just such a clod of earth, decomposing and dissolving in the grave. So to believe that a human being can be made out of what we then have before us is really just as great a folly.

You see, on the one hand people claim nowadays that it is incorrect to suppose that the human being could be formed from a lump of earth; on the other hand one is allowed to believe that he consists of earth alone. If one wants to be logical, then the one is no better than the other. One must be clear that while a person lives there is something in him that gives him shape and form, and when it is no longer in him he can no longer keep his form. The forces of nature do not give him this form but merely break it down, they do not make it grow. So we must look instead to the soul and spirit of a person, which really hold sway as long as he is living.

Now when we look at a lifeless stone, if we imagine that it has always been the same as it is today, that is just as if we would say a corpse had always been as it is even while the human being was alive. The stones that we see today in the world outside, the rocks, the mountains, are just the same as a corpse; in fact, they *are* a corpse! They were not always as they are today. Just as a human corpse was not always what it is once the soul and spirit have gone, so what we see outside has not always been in its present condition. The fact that plants grow on the lifeless corpse, that is, on the rocks, need not surprise us; for when a human corpse decays, all sorts of tiny plants and tiny animals grow out of it.

Of course, what is outside in nature seems beautiful, and what we see on a corpse when all sorts of parasitic plants are growing out of it does not seem beautiful. But that is only because the one is gigantic in size and the other is small. If we were not human beings but were tiny beetles crawling about on a decaying corpse and could think like human beings, we would regard the bones of the corpse as rocks. We would consider what was decayed as rubble and stones; we would—since we were tiny beetles—see great forests in what was growing on the corpse; we would have a whole world to admire and not think it revolting as we do now.

Just as we must go back to what a person was before he died, so in the case of the earth and our surroundings we must go back to what once lived in all that today is lifeless, before indeed the earth as a whole died. If the earth as a whole had not died there could be no human being. Human beings are parasites, as it were, on the present earth. The whole earth was once alive; it could think as you and I now think. But only when it became a corpse could it produce the human race. This is something we can all realize if we think about it. But people today do not want to think. Yet one must think if one wishes to get to the truth.

We have, therefore, to imagine that what is today solid rock with plants growing, and so on, was originally entirely different. Originally there was a living, thinking, cosmic body—a living, thinking, cosmic body!

What do people today imagine? They imagine that originally there was a gigantic mist, that this primeval mist started spinning, that the planets then split off, that the sun became the centre. This is taught to children quite early on, and a little experiment is made to show that everything really did start in that way. A few drops of oil are put in a glass of water; one lets the oil swim on the water. A piece of cardboard has a pin stuck through it; then with the pin one makes the cardboard revolve; little oil-drops split off, go on revolving, and a tiny planetary system actually forms with the sun in the centre.[1]

Well now, it is usually quite a virtue if one can forget oneself, but in this case the teacher should not! When he makes the experiment, he ought then to say to the children: 'Out there in the universe is a giant schoolteacher who did the rotating!'

What it amounts to is thoughtlessness — not because the facts oblige one to be thoughtless, but because one wants to be. But that doesn't help one reach the truth.

We must therefore imagine not that a gigantic schoolteacher was there who rotated the world mist, but that there was something in the world mist itself that was able to move and so on. In doing so we return to real, living forces. If we want to rotate, we don't need a pin stuck through us with which a teacher rotates us. That's not for us; we can rotate ourselves. This schoolroom variety of primeval mist would have to be rotated by a schoolteacher. But if it is living and can feel and think, then it needs no cosmic schoolteacher; it can cause the rotation itself.

So we must picture that what today is lifeless around us was once alive, was sensitive, was a cosmic being. If we look further, there were even a great number of cosmic beings animating the whole. The original conditions of the world are therefore due to the fact that there was spirit within the substance.

Now what is it that underlies everything material? Imagine that I have a lump of lead in my hand, in other words solid matter, thoroughly solid matter. Now if I put this lead on red-hot iron or on anything red-hot, on fire, it turns to fluid. If I work on it still further with fire, the whole lead vanishes; it evaporates, and I see nothing more of it. It is the same with all substances. On what does it depend, then, that a substance is solid? It depends upon the degree of warmth it contains. The appearance of a substance depends only upon how much warmth is in it.

You know, today one can make the air liquid, then one has liquid air. The air we have in our surroundings is only airy, gaseous, as long as it contains a definite amount of warmth. And water — water is fluid, but it can also become ice and therefore solid. If there were a certain cold temperature everywhere on our earth there would be no water, but only ice. Now let us examine our mountains; there we find solid granite or other solid rock. But if it were immensely hot there, there would be no solid granite; it would be fluid and flow away like the water in our brooks.

What then is the original element that makes things solid or fluid or gaseous? It is heat! And unless heat is there in the first place, nothing at all can be solid or fluid. So we can say that heat or fire is what underlies everything in the beginning.

That is also shown by the research of spiritual science or anthroposophy. Spiritual science shows that originally there was not a primeval mist, a lifeless mist, but that living warmth was there at the beginning, simple living *warmth*. Thus I will assume an original cosmic body that was living warmth. [See drawing — red.] In my *Occult Science* I have called this original warmth condition the Saturn condition; it has been called this from ancient times, and though one must have a name, it is not the name that matters. It has, in fact, something to do with the planet Saturn, but we will not go into that now.

In this original condition there were as yet no solid bodies and no air, only warmth; but the warmth was living. When you freeze today, it's your ego that freezes; when you sweat today, it's your ego that sweats, that becomes thoroughly

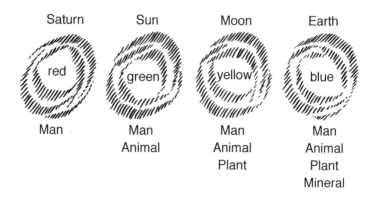

Saturn	Sun	Moon	Earth
red	green	yellow	blue
Man	Man	Man	Man
	Animal	Animal	Animal
		Plant	Plant
			Mineral

hot. You are always at some temperature: sometimes heat, sometimes cold, but always in some kind of temperature. In fact, we can still see today that the human being lives in warmth. The human being lives absolutely in warmth.

When modern science says that originally there was great heat, in a certain sense it is right; but when it thinks that this great heat was lifeless, then it is wrong. A living cosmic being was present, a thoroughly living cosmic being.

Now the first thing to happen to this warmth-being was a cooling down. Things cool down continually. And what happens when what has been nothing but warmth now cools down? Air arises, air, the gaseous state. For when we go on heating a solid object, gas is formed in the warmth; but when something not yet substance cools down from above downwards, air is formed at first. So we can say that the second condition to come about was gaseous, definitely airy. [See drawing—green.]

In what has been formed, in a certain sense, as a second cosmic body, everything is air. There is as yet no water, nothing solid within it; it consists entirely of air.

So now we have the second condition that formed itself in the course of time. You see, in this second condition something else developed along with what was already there. I have called this second condition 'Sun' in my *Occult*

Science; it was not the present sun, but a sunlike condition, a warm air-mist. The present sun, as I have told you, is not that, nor is it what was originally this second cosmic body. Thus we get a second planetary body formed out of the first; the first was pure warmth, the second was airy in nature.

Now in warmth the human soul can live. Warmth impresses feeling on the soul and does not destroy it. It destroys the body, however; if I were thrown into the fire my body would be destroyed but not my soul. (We will speak of this in more detail later, for naturally the question needs to be considered carefully.) For this reason the human being could already live as soul during the first, the Saturn, condition. But although man could live then, the animal could not, for when an animal's body is destroyed the soul element is also affected. Fire has an influence on the soul of the animal. In the first condition, therefore, man is present but not the animal.

When the transformation had taken place that gave rise to the Sun condition [see drawing], both human being and animal were there. That is the important fact. It is not true that the animals were there originally and that man developed out of them. Man was there originally and afterwards the animals evolved out of what could not become man. Naturally the human being was not going about on two feet when there was only warmth—obviously not. He lived in the warmth and was a floating being; he possessed only a condition of warmth. Then, as this metamorphosed into an air-warmth body, the animals were formed and appeared beside man. Thus the animals are indeed related to man, but they developed only later in the course of world evolution.

Now how did things continue? The warmth decreased, and as it gradually decreased, not only was air formed but also water. Thus we have a third cosmic body. [See drawing—yellow.] I have called it 'Moon' because it was slightly similar to our present moon, although it was not our present moon. It was a watery, a thoroughly watery body. Air and warmth naturally remained, but now water appeared which had not been present in the second condition. After the appearance of water, man and the animals were joined by plants pushing up out of the water. Plants originally grew in water, not in earth. So we have man, animal, plant.

You see, plants seem to grow out of the earth, but if the earth contained no water, no plants would grow; they need water for their growth. There are also, as you know, aquatic plants, and you can think of the original plants as being similar to these; the original plants swam in the water. The animals too you must picture as swimming animals and in the former, second condition, even as flying animals.

Something still actually remains of all that was there originally. During the Sun condition, when only man and animal were in existence, everything had to fly, and since the air has remained and still exists, those flying creatures have their descendants. Our present birds are the descendants of the original animals that developed during the Sun condition. However, at that time they were not as they are today. Those animal creatures consisted purely of air; they were airy clouds. Later [Moon condition] they had water in them. Today—let us look at a bird. Usually a bird is observed very thoughtlessly. If we are to picture the animals as they existed during the Sun condition, we must say that they consisted only of air; they were hovering air-clouds. When we look at a bird today, we should realize that it has hollow bones filled with air. It is very interesting to see that in the present bird. There is air everywhere in this bird, in the bones, everywhere! Think away whatever is not air and you get an air-being—the bird. If it did not have this air, it could not fly at all. It has hollow bones; within, it is an air-bird, reminding us of former conditions. The rest of the body was built around it in later times. The birds are really the descendants of the Sun condition.

Look at modern man: he can live in the air, but he can't fly; he is too heavy to fly. He has not formed hollow bones for himself like the bird, or else he too could fly. Then he would not just have shoulder-blades, but his shoulder-blades would stretch out into wings. The human being still has the rudiments of wings up there in his shoulder-blades; if these were to grow out, he would be able to fly.

Thus man lives in the air surrounding him. But this air must contain vapour. Man cannot live in purely dry air; he needs fluids.

There is a condition, however, in which the human being cannot live in the air: that is the very earliest human state, the embryo. One must look at these things rightly. During the embryonic period the human germ or embryo obtains air and all that it needs from the body of the mother. It must be enclosed in something living.

You see, it is like this. If the human embryo is removed by operation from the body of the mother, it cannot yet live in the air. During the embryonic condition the human being needs to be sustained by living surroundings. At the time when man, animal and plant existed, but as yet no stones or minerals as we have them today, everything was alive and the human being lived surrounded by what was alive just as now he lives as embryo in the mother's body. Naturally he grew bigger. Think of this: if we did not have to be born and live in the air and breathe on our own, then our span of life would end with our birth. As embryo we could all live only ten moon-months. As a matter of fact, there are such creatures that live only ten months; these do not come to the outer air but get air from within a living environment. So it was with the human being a long time ago. He certainly grew older, but he never left the living element. He lived in that state all the time. He did not advance to birth; he lived as embryo. At that time there were as yet no minerals, no rocks.

If the body of a human being is dissected today, the same carbonate of lime will be found in his bones as you find here in the Jura Mountains. There is now a mineral substance inside the body that was not present in the earlier evolutionary condition. In the embryo too, particularly in the first months, there is no deposit of mineral; everything is still fluid, only slightly thickened. And so it was during this earlier condition; man was not yet bony, having at most cartilage. Of such a human being we are reminded today only by the human embryo. Why cannot the human embryo come immediately out of the mother's body? Because the world today is a different world. As long as Old Moon lasted—I will now call it Old Moon, as it is not the present moon but the former state of the earth—as long as the Old Moon period lasted, the whole earth was a womb, inwardly alive, a real womb. There was nothing yet of stone or mineral. It was all a gigantic womb, and we can say that our present earth came forth from this gigantic womb.

Previously this immense womb did not exist at all. What was it then? Well, in fact, at an earlier stage there was something else in existence. Let us just consider what came before. You see, if a human being is to develop in the mother's body, if he is to be an embryo, he must first be conceived. The conception takes place. But does nothing precede conception? What precedes conception is the monthly period in the woman; that is what comes first. A very special process takes place in the female organism that is connected with the expulsion of blood. But that is not the only thing; that is only the physical aspect. Every time this blood is expelled something of a spiritual-soul nature is born at the same time, and this remains. It does not become physical, because no conception has taken place. The spiritual-soul element remains without becoming a physical human body. What a human being requires before conception was also there during the cosmic Sun condition! The whole Sun was a cosmic being that from time to time expelled something spiritual. So man and animal lived in the airlike condition, thrust out, expelled by this whole body. Between one condition (Sun) and the other (Moon), the human being became a physical being in water. Formerly he was a physical being only in air. During this Moon condition we have something similar to conception, but not yet anything similar to birth. What was the nature of this conception during the ancient Moon condition?

The Moon was there, an entirely female being, and in polarity to it was not a male being, but all that was still outside its planetary body at that time. Outside it were many other planetary bodies that exerted an influence. Now comes the drawing which I have already made here.

So this planetary body was there and around it the other planetary bodies, exerting their influence in the most varied ways. Seeds came in from outside and fertilized the whole Moon-earth. And if you could have lived at that time and set foot on this primeval cosmic body, you would not have said when you saw all sorts of drops coming in, 'It is raining', as one says today. At that time you would have said, 'Earth is being fertilized.' There were seasons when the fructifying seeds came in from all directions, and other seasons when they matured and no more arrived. Thus at that time there was a cosmic fertilization. But the human being was not born, only fertilized; he was only called forth by conception. The human being came out of the entire body of the earth, or Moon-body as it was then. In the same way fertilization of animal and plant came from the whole cosmic surroundings.

Now later, through further cooling, there came about a hardening of all that lived then as man, animal and plant. There, in the Moon condition, everything is still water, though later on a certain hardening occurs through cooling. Here on the earth the solid, the mineral appears. So now we have a fourth condition [see drawing]: this is our earth as we have it today, and it contains man, animal, plant, mineral.

Let us just look at what the bird, for instance, has become on the earth. During this time (Sun condition) the bird was still a sort of air-sack; it consisted of nothing but air, a mass of air floating along. Then during this time (Moon condition) it became watery, a thickened watery thing, and it hovered as a kind of cloud — not like our clouds, though, but already containing a form. What for us are only formless water structures were at that time forms. There was a skeleton form, but it was fluid. But now came the mineral element, and this was incorporated into what was only water structure. Carbonate of lime, phosphatic lime, and so on formed along the skeleton, creating solid bones. So at first we have the air-bird, then the water-bird, and at last the solid earth-bird.

This could not be the same in the case of the human being. Man could not simply incorporate into himself what only arose as mineral during his embryonic period. The bird could do this — and why? You see, the bird acquired its air form here (Sun condition); it then lived through the water condition. It is essential for it not to let the mineral come too close to it during its germinal state. If the mineral came to it too soon, then it would just become a mineral and harden. The bird while it is developing is still somewhat watery and fluid; the mineral, however, tries to approach. What does the bird do? Well, it pushes it off, it makes something around itself, it makes the eggshell around itself! That is the mineral element. The eggshell remains as long as the bird must protect itself inwardly from the mineral; that is, as long as it must stay fluid. The reason for this is that the bird originated only during the second condition of the earth. If it had been there during the first condition, it would now be much more sensitive to warmth than it actually is. Since it was not there at that time, it can now form the hard eggshell around itself.

The human being was already present during the first condition of the earth, the warmth condition, and therefore he cannot now hold off the mineral while he is in the embryonic stage. He can't build an eggshell; he must be organized differently. He must take up the mineral element from the womb, and so we have mineral formation already at the end of embryonic development. The human being must absorb some mineral from the womb; therefore the womb must first possess the mineral that is to be absorbed. So in the case of the human being the mineral element is incorporated quite differently. The bird has air-filled bones; we human beings have marrow-filled bones, very different from the bones of the bird. Through the fact of our having this marrow a human mother is able to provide mineral substance to the embryo within her. But once the mineral element is provided, the human being is no longer able to live in the womb environment and must gradually be born. He must first have acquired mineral constituents. With the bird it is not a matter of being born, but of creeping out of the eggshell; man is born without an eggshell. Why? Because man originated earlier and therefore everything can be done through warmth and not through air.

From this you can understand the differences that still exist and that can be observed today. The difference between an 'egg-animal' and such a being as man, and also the higher mammals, lies in the fact that the human being is far older than, for instance, the bird species, far older than the minerals. Therefore, when he is developing during the embryonic stage in the womb, he must be protected from mineral nature and may only be given the prepared mineral that comes from the mother. In fact, the mineral element prepared in the mother's body must still be given to him for a certain period after birth in the mother's milk! While the bird can be fed at once with external substances, man and the higher animals can only be nourished by what the mother's body provides.

What we receive today, in our present Earth condition, from the mother's body, we received during the previous cosmic condition from the air, from the environment. What we had around us then during our whole life was like milk. Our air today contains oxygen and nitrogen but relatively little carbon and hydrogen and particularly very, very little sulphur. They have gone. During the Moon condition it was different; in the surrounding air there were not only oxygen and nitrogen but also hydrogen, carbon, sulphur. That made a sort of milky pap around the Moon, a quite thin milk-pap in which life existed. Today man still lives in a thin milk-pap before he is born! For it is only after his birth that the milk goes into the breast; before birth it passes to those parts of the female body where the human embryo is lying. That is an amazing thing, that processes in the mother's organism that belong to the uterus before birth afterwards pass to the breast. And so the Moon condition is still preserved in man before he is born, and the actual Earth condition only comes at the moment of birth, with Moon-nature still present in the breast milk.

This is how things connected with the origin of the earth and mankind must be explained. If people do not find a spiritual-scientific way of looking at things they simply cannot solve the mystery of why a bird slips out of an egg and can at once be nourished with external substances, while a human being cannot slip out of an egg and must come out of the womb to be nourished by mother's milk. Why is it? It is because the bird originated later and is thus an external being. Man originated earlier, and when he was undergoing the Moon condition, he was not yet as hardened as the bird. Hence today too he is not yet so hardened; he must still be more protected, for he has within him much more of the original conditions.

Since people today on the whole can no longer think properly, they misunderstand what exists on earth as plant, animal and man. Thus materialistic Darwinism arose, which believed that the animals were there first and that man simply developed out of the animals. It is true that in his external form man is related to the animals, but he existed earlier, and the animals really developed later after the world had gone through a transformation. And so we can say that the animals we see now present a later stage of an earlier condition when they were indeed more closely related to man. But we must never allow ourselves to imagine that out of the present animals a human being could arise. That is a thoroughly false idea.

Now let us look not at the bird species but at the fishes. The bird species developed for the air, the fish species for the water. Not until what we call the Moon condition were certain earlier, airlike bird-beings transformed in such a way as to become fishlike—because of the water. To the birdlike beings were added the fish. One could say that the fish are birds that have become watery, birds received by the water. You can gather from this that the fish appeared later than the birds; they appeared when the watery element was there, that is, during the Old Moon period.

And now you will no longer be astonished that everything swimming about in a watery state during the Old Moon time looked fishlike. The birds looked fishlike in spite of flying in the air and being lighter. Everything was fishlike. Now this is interesting: if we look today at a human embryo at about the 21st or 22nd day after conception, how does it appear? There it swims in a fluid element in the mother's body, and it really looks like a tiny fish! The human being actually had this form during the ancient

Moon period and he has it still in the third week of pregnancy; he has preserved it.

You can say, then, that the human being develops himself
out of this Old Moon form, and we can still see by the fish
form he has in the embryo how he has developed. When we
observe the world as it is today we can see how everything
used to be full of life, just as we know that a corpse was once
alive. So today I have described to you the earlier condition
of what we now have on earth as mineral. We look at a
corpse and say that it can no longer move its legs, its hands,
no longer open its mouth or eyes — everything has become
immobile; yet that leads us back to a human state when
everything could be moved — legs, arms, hands — when the
eyes could be opened. In just the same way we look around
us at the corpse of the earth, the remains of a living body, in
which man and animal still wander about, and we look
back to the time when the entire earth was once alive.

But there is something more. I said that with conception
the potentiality of the physical human being is there, and
gradually the embryo develops. I also described what
happens before this, the processes in the female organism,
what is expelled in the monthly periods, and how a spiritual element is pushed out too. Now in this process there is
always something of the nature of fever, even in a perfectly
normal, healthy woman. This is because it represents a
warmth condition; it is the warmth condition that has been
preserved from the ancient first condition that we have in
the drawing I have called Saturn. This fever condition still
endures.

One can say that the whole of our evolution proceeded
from a kind of fever condition of our earth, which the
cooling down finally brought to an end. Most people today
are no longer feverish but thoroughly dry and matter-of-
fact. Yet even now, when there is something not caused by
outside warmth but appearing inwardly as warmth, giving

us something similar to an inward life, now too we have a condition of fever.

So it is, gentlemen: one sees everywhere in the conditions of present mankind how they can be traced back to conditions of the past. Today I have told you how man, animal, plant and mineral gradually evolved as the entire planetary body on which they developed grew more and more solid.

We will speak further of all this—today is Monday—on Wednesday at nine o'clock.[2]

Creation of the earth — origin of the human being

Rudolf Steiner: Good morning, gentlemen! Today I would like to speak further about the creation of the earth and the origin of man. It has surely become clear from what I have already said that the earth was originally not what it is today, but was a kind of living being.

I described the condition that existed before our present Earth condition by saying that warmth, air, and water were there but as yet no really solid mineral structures. Now you must not imagine that the water existing at that time looked like the water we know today. Our present water has become what it is through separation from it of certain substances which were formerly dissolved in it. If you take a glass of ordinary water and put some salt in it, the salt dissolves in the water and you get a fluid — a salt solution, as one calls it — which is denser than the original water. If you put your fingers in it, it feels much denser than water. Now dissolved salt is relatively thin; with certain other substances one gets quite a thickish liquid.

The fluid condition, the watery condition which existed in earlier ages of our earth was therefore not that of today's water. That did not exist, for all substances were dissolved in the water. All the substances that you have today — the Jura limestone mountains, for instance — were dissolved; harder rocks that you can't scratch with a knife (limestone can always be scratched) were also dissolved in the water. During this Old Moon stage, therefore, we are talking of a thickish fluid that contained in solution all the substances which today are solid.

The thin water of today, which consists essentially of

hydrogen and oxygen, was separated off later; it has developed only during the Earth period itself. Thus we have as an original condition of the earth a densified fluid, and round about it a kind of air. But this was not the air of today; just as the water was not like our present water, so the air was not the same as our present air. Our present air essentially contains oxygen and nitrogen; other substances which it still contains are present to a very slight degree. There are even metals still present in the air, but in exceedingly small quantities. For instance there is one metal, sodium, that is everywhere in the air. Just think what that means — that sodium is everywhere, that a substance which is in the salt on your table is present everywhere in tiny quantities.

There are two substances — one is the sodium which I have just mentioned, which is present in small quantities in the air; then there is a substance of a gaseous nature which plays a great role when you bleach your laundry: chlorine. It causes bleaching. Now the salt on your table is composed of sodium and chlorine, a combination of the two. Such things come about in nature.

You can ask how one knows that sodium is everywhere. It is possible today to tell from a flame what sort of substance is being burnt in it. For instance, you can get sodium in a metallic form and pulverize it and hold it in a flame. You can then find with an instrument called a spectroscope that there is a yellow line in it. There is another metal, for example, called lithium; if you hold that in the flame, you get a red line; the yellow is no longer there, but there is a red line. One can prove with the spectroscope what substance is present.

But you get the yellow sodium line in almost every flame whenever you light one, without having put the sodium in yourself. Thus sodium is still in the air today. In earlier times immense quantities of metals and even of sulphur were present in the air. The air was quite saturated with sulphur. So there was a thickish water — if one had not been especially heavy one could have gone for a walk on it; it was like melted tar — and there was a dense air, so dense that one could not have breathed in it with our present lungs. These were only formed later. The mode of life of the creatures that existed at that time was utterly different.

Now you must picture to yourselves that the earth once looked like this. [See drawing.] Had you found yourself there with your present eyes, you would not have discovered the stars and sun and moon out there, for you would have looked out into a vague ocean of air which reached an end eventually. If one could have lived then with our present sense organs, one would have seemed to be inside a world-egg beyond which one could see nothing. And you can imagine how different the earth looked at that time, like a kind of giant egg yolk, a thick fluid, and a thick air environment corresponding to the white of the present-day egg.

If you picture concretely what I have described, you will have to say: Well, creatures such as we have today could not have lived at that time. Naturally, creatures like the elephant, and even human beings in their present form, would have sunk — nor could they have breathed. And because they could not have breathed, there were also no lungs as we know them now. Organs are formed entirely according to the function they are needed for. It is very interesting that an organ is simply not there if it is not needed. And so lungs only developed when the air was no longer so full of sulphur and metals as it had been in those ancient times.

Now to get an idea of what sort of creatures lived at that time, we must first look for those that lived in the thickish water. Creatures lived in that dense water that no longer exist today. Our present fish have their form because the water is thin. Even sea-water is comparatively thin; it contains much salt in solution, yet it is comparatively thin. But in that early time every possible substance was dissolved in the dense fluid, the dense ocean, of which, in fact, the whole earth, the Moon-egg consisted.

The creatures that were in it could not swim in our sense, because the water was too thick; nor could they walk, for one needs firm ground for walking. You can imagine that these creatures had a bodily structure somewhere between what one needs for swimming—fins—and what one needs for walking—feet. You know, of course, what a fin looks like—it has quite fine, spiky bones and the flesh in between is dried-up. So that a fin has practically no flesh on it, and prickly bones transformed to spikes: that is a fin. Limbs that are suitable for moving forward on firm ground, that is, for walking or crawling, have their bones set into the interior and the outer bulk of flesh covers them. We can therefore regard such limbs as having flesh outside and bones inside; there the bulk of flesh is the main thing. This is what we need for walking or swimming.

But at that time there was neither walking nor swimming, but something in between. These creatures therefore had limbs in which there was something of a thornlike nature, but also something like joints. They were really quite ingenious joints, and in between, the flesh mass was stretched out like an umbrella. You still see many swimming creatures today with a 'swim skin' — a web — between the bones, and they are the last relics of what once existed in vast numbers. Creatures existed which stretched out their limbs so that the spreading flesh mass was supported by the dense fluid. And they had joints in their limbs — the fishes today have none — and with these they could direct their half-swimming, half-walking.

Such animals chiefly needed such limbs. Today these limbs would look immensely coarse and clumsy; they were not fins, not feet, not hands, but clumsy appendages on the body, thoroughly appropriate for living in that thick fluid. This was one kind of animal. If we want to describe them further, we must say that they especially developed these immense limbs. All the rest of them was poorly developed. If you look at the toads and similar creatures existing today which swim in thick boggy marshes, then you have a faint, miniature reminder of the gigantic animals which lived once upon a time, which were heavy and clumsy but had diminutive heads like turtles.

Other creatures lived in the dense air. Our present birds have had to acquire what they need to live in our thin air; they have had to develop something of a lung nature. But the creatures that lived at that time in the air had no lungs; in that dense sulphurous air it would not have been possible to breathe with lungs. They absorbed the air as a kind of food. They could not have eaten in the present way, for it would all have remained lying in the stomach. Nor was there anything solid there to eat. All that they took in as food they took from the densified air. Where did they direct this nourishment? Well, into what had especially developed within them.

Now the flesh masses that existed in those gliding creatures (for they were not really walking and not really swimming) could not be used by the air-creatures, for these had to support themselves in the air, not swim in the dense fluid. So the flesh masses which had developed in the gliding, half-swimming creatures became adapted to the sulphurous condition of the air. The sulphur dried up these flesh masses and made them into what you see today as birds' feathers. With this flesh mass or dried-up tissue the creatures could form the limbs they needed. They were not wings in today's sense, but they supported them in the air, and were something similar to the wings of today. They were very, very different in one respect: there is only one thing remaining from these winglike structures, and that is moulting, when our present birds lose their feathers. These former creatures supported themselves in the dense air with the structures that were not yet feathers but rather dried-up tissue.

Moreover, these structures were actually half for breathing and half for taking in nourishment. What existed in the air environment was absorbed. These organs were not used for flying; these rudimentary 'wings' were for absorbing the air and pushing it away. Today only moulting is left of this process. At that time, these structures served for taking in nourishment; that is, the bird puffed up its tissue with what it absorbed from the air and then gave out again what it did not need. So such a bird had a very remarkable structure indeed!

And so at that time there lived those terribly clumsy creatures below in the water-element — our present turtles are indeed fine princes by comparison! And above were these remarkable creatures. And whereas our present birds sometimes behave rather inconsiderately towards us as they fly (which we object to), the birdlike creatures in the air of that time excreted continuously. What came from them rained down, and rained down especially at certain times. The creatures below did not yet have the attitude which we have. We are indignant if a bird sometimes behaves in an unseemly way. But those creatures below in the fluid element were not displeased; they sucked up into their own bodies what fell down from above. That was the fertilizing process at that time. That was the only way in which these creatures which had originated there could continue to live. In those ages there was no definite reproduction of one animal from another, as we have now. One might say that actually these creatures lived a long time; they kept renewing themselves. One could call it a sort of cosmic moulting; the animals down below kept rejuvenating themselves again and again.

On the other hand, to the creatures above came what was developed by those below and this again was a kind of fertilizing. Reproduction was at that time of a very different nature; it went on in the whole earth-body. The upper world fertilized the lower, the lower world fertilized the upper. The whole earth-body was alive. One could say that the creatures below and the creatures above were like maggots in a body — where the whole body is alive and the maggots in it are alive too. It was one life, and the various beings lived in a completely living body.

But later something occurred, a condition of very special importance. The condition I have described could have gone on for a long time; all could have remained as it was without becoming our present earth. The heavy, clumsy creatures could have continued to inhabit the living earth together with the creatures able to live in the air. But one day something happened. It happened that one day from this living earth, let me say, an offspring was formed and went out into cosmic space. It came about in this way: a small protuberance developed, which withered away at one place [see drawing] and at last split off. And a body was now out in the universe which had, instead of the earlier conditions, the surrounding air inside and the thick fluid outside. Thus an inverted body separated off. Whereas the

Moon-earth remained with thick fluid for its inner nucleus and thickish air outside, a body split off which now had the thicker substance outside and the thinner inside. And if one investigates the matter without prejudice, in honest research, one can recognize in this body the present moon. Today just as one can find sodium in the air, one can also learn the exact constituents of the moon, and so one can know that the moon was once in the earth. What circles round us out there was formerly within the earth, then separated off and went out into the cosmos.

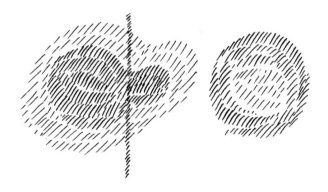

With this a complete change took place, not only in what separated itself off but also in the earth itself. Above all, the earth lost certain substances, and for the first time the mineral element could be formed in the earth. If the moon-substances had remained in the earth, minerals could never have formed, and there would always have been a state of moving fluid. The departure of the moon brought death for the first time to the earth and with it the dead mineral kingdom. But with this came also the possibility for the plants, animals and man to develop in their present form.

We can say, therefore, that out of the Old Moon arose the present earth together with the mineral kingdom. And now all forms had to alter. For with the departure of the moon the air became less sulphurous, was closer to present conditions, and what had been dissolved in the fluid was now expelled, forming mountain-like masses. The water grew more and more like our present water. On the other hand the moon, which has around it what we have in the interior of the earth, produced a thickish, horny mass on the outside. This is what we see when we look up. It is not like our mineral kingdom, but it is as if our mineral kingdom had become hornlike and turned into glass. It is extraordinarily hard, harder than anything hornlike that we have on earth, but it is not quite mineral. Hence the peculiar shape of the moon mountains; they actually all look like horns that have been fastened on. They are formed in such a way that one can even perceive what had been organic in them, what had once been a part of life.

Beginning with the separation of the moon, our present minerals were gradually deposited out of the former dense fluid. Particularly active was a substance that in those ancient times existed in great amounts and consisted of silica and oxygen—we call it silicic acid. One has the idea that an acid must be fluid, because that is the form in which it is used today. But the acid which I mean here and which is a genuine acid is extremely hard and firm. It is, in fact, quartz! The quartz which you find in the high mountains is silicic acid. And when it is whitish and like glass it is pure silicic acid. If it contains other substances you get the types of quartz that look violet, and so on. That comes from the substances contained in it.

But the quartz which is so hard today that you can't scratch it with a knife, and if you hit your head on it, it would make a real hole in your head—this same quartz was dissolved in those ancient times, either in the thick fluid or in the finer surroundings of dense air. In addition to the sulphur there was an immense amount of dissolved quartz in the thick air around the earth. You can get an idea of the strong influence this dissolved silicic acid had at that time if you reflect on the composition of the earth today just here where we live. Of course you can say: There must be a great deal of oxygen, because we need it for breathing. Yes, there is a good deal of oxygen: 28 to 29% of the whole volume of the earth. You have to count everything. Oxygen is in the air and in many solid substances on the earth too; it is in the plants and animals. And if you put all this together it is 28% of the whole.

But silica, which when united with oxygen in the quartz gives silicic acid, makes up 48 to 49%! Think what that means: half of all that surrounds us and that we need, almost half of that is silica! When everything was fluid, when the air was almost fluid before it thickened — yes, then this silica played an enormous role, it was very important in that original condition. Nowadays these things are not understood rightly because people no longer have the right idea about the human being's finer organization. They think today in a casual, crude way: 'Well, we're humans and we have to breathe. We breathe oxygen in and we breathe carbon dioxide out. We can't live if we don't breathe like this.' But silica is still always contained in the air we inhale, genuine silica, tiny quantities of silica. Plenty is available, for 48 to 49% of our surroundings are made up of silica.

When we breathe, the oxygen descends into the metabolism and unites with carbon, but at the same time it also goes up to the senses and the brain, to the nervous system; it goes everywhere. There it unites with the silica and forms silicic acid in us. If we look at a human being we see he has lungs and is inhaling air; that means he is taking in oxygen. Below, the oxygen unites with carbon and forms carbon dioxide which we then exhale. But above, the silica is united in us with the oxygen and goes up into our head as silicic acid — however, it does not become as solid up there as quartz. That, of course, would be a bad business if pure quartz crystals showed up inside your head—then instead of hair you would have quartz crystals, which perhaps would be quite beautiful and amusing! Still, that is not entirely fantasy—for there is a good deal of silicic acid in our hair, only it is still fluid, not crystallized. In fact, not only hair but practically everything in the nerves and senses contains silicic acid.

One discovers this when one first gets to know the beneficial, healing effects of silicic acid; it is tremendously helpful as a remedy. You must realize that the food received through the mouth into the stomach must pass through all manner of intermediate things before it comes up into the head, the eye, the ear, and so forth. That is a long way for the nourishment to go, and it needs helping forces to enable it to reappear there at all. It might be—in fact it happens often—that a person has not enough helping forces and the foods do not work their way properly into the head; then one must prescribe silicic acid which assists the nourishment to rise to the head and the senses. As soon as one sees that a patient is normal as regards stomach and intestines, but that the digestion does not go all the way to the sense organs, the head, or the skin, one must administer a silicic acid preparation as remedy. There one sees, in fact, what a very great role silicic acid still plays today in the human organism.

In that ancient condition of the earth, the silicic acid was not yet inhaled but was absorbed. The birdlike creatures in particular took it in. They absorbed it as they absorbed the sulphur, with the consequence that they became almost entirely sense organs. Just as we have silicic acid to thank for our sense organs, so at that time the earth as a whole owed its birdlike species to the working of the silicic acid that was present everywhere. Since, however, this did not come in the same way to those other creatures with the clumsy limbs, since the silicic acid reached those creatures less as they glided along in the dense fluid, they became in the main stomach- and digestion-creatures. The creatures in the sky above in those days were terribly nervous creatures, aware of everything with a fine nervous sensitivity. On the other hand, those below in the thick fluid were of immense sagacity, but also immensely phlegmatic. They felt nothing of it; they were mere feeding-creatures, were really only an abdomen with clumsy limbs. The birds above were finely organized, were almost entirely sense organs. And indeed they were sense organs for the earth itself, so that it was not only filled with life but it perceived everything through these sense organs that were in the air, the forerunners of our birds.

I tell you all this so that you may see how different everything once looked on the earth. All that was dissolved at that time became deposits later in the solid mineral mountains, the rock masses, and formed a kind of bony scaffolding. Only then was it possible for man and animal to form solid bones. For when externally the bony framework of the earth was formed, then bones began to form also inside the higher animals and man. What I have spoken of before was not yet firm, hard bone as we have today, but flexible, hornlike cartilage as it has still remained in the fish. All these things have in a certain way remained behind and atrophied, for in the earlier ages which I have described the life-conditions for them were there, but today the necessary life-conditions are no longer present. We can say, therefore, that our modern birds are successors to the birdlike species which existed above in the dense air full of sulphur and silicic acid, but now transformed and adapted to the present air. And the amphibians of today, the crawling creatures, the frogs and toads, but also the chameleon, snake, and so forth, are successors to the creatures that were swimming at that time in the dense fluid. The higher mammals and man in his present form came later.

Now this makes an apparent contradiction. I said to you last time that man was there first. But he lived in the warmth purely as soul and spirit; he was indeed already present in all that I have described, but not as a physical being. He was there in a very fine body in which he could support himself equally in the air and in the dense fluid. And neither he nor the higher mammals were visible as yet; only the heavy creatures and the birdlike air-creatures were visible. That is what must be distinguished when one says that man was already there. He was first of all, before even the air was there, but he was invisible, and he was still in an invisible state when the earth appeared as I have now described. The moon had first to separate from the earth, then man could deposit mineral elements in himself, could form a mineral bony system, could develop such substances as protein, and so forth, in his muscles. At that time such substances did not as yet exist. Nevertheless, man has completely preserved in his present corporeal nature the legacy of those earlier times.

For the human being cannot now come into existence without the moon influence, which now emanates only from without. Reproduction is connected with the moon, though no longer directly. It can therefore be seen that what is connected with reproduction—the woman's monthly periods—take their course in the same rhythmical periods as the phases of the moon, only they no longer coincide; they have freed themselves. But the moon influence has remained active in human reproduction.

We have found reproduction accomplished between the beings of the dense air and those of the dense fluid, between the birdlike race and the ancient giant amphibians. They mutually fertilized one another because the moon was still within the earth. As soon as the moon was outside, fertilization had to come from outside, because the fertilizing principle lies in the moon.

We will continue from this point on Saturday[3] at nine
o'clock — if we can have that hour. The question put by Herr
Dollinger is one that must be answered in detail, and if you
have patience you will see how present-day life emerges
from all the gradual preparatory conditions. The whole
subject is indeed difficult to understand. But I believe one
can understand if one looks at things in the way we have
been looking.

What anthroposophy and science have to say about earth strata and fossils

Rudolf Steiner: Good morning, gentlemen! You will have realized from all we've said that our earth in its present form is only the last remains of what was once essentially different. If we want to compare its earlier condition with anything, we can only compare it really—as you have seen—with what one has in an egg cell. Our earth today has a solid core of all sorts of minerals and metals. And we have the air around us, and in the air two substances which especially affect us—we could not live without them: oxygen and nitrogen. We can say therefore that in the earth we have a hard core of all kinds of substances, 70 to 80 of them, and around us the sheath of air containing mainly nitrogen and oxygen.

Nitrogen and oxygen, however, are only the main constituents. The air always contains other substances, though in very small quantities, such as carbon, hydrogen, sulphur, among others. But these are also the substances contained in the white of an egg, in the white of a hen's egg. Oxygen, nitrogen, hydrogen, carbon and sulphur! The difference is merely that in the egg-white the sulphur, hydrogen and carbon are closely combined with the oxygen and nitrogen, while in the outer air they are present in a much looser way. So the same substances are in the air that are in the hen's egg. The same substances are present in a much smaller amount in the yolk, and we can therefore say that when it hardens, densifies, it becomes what the earth is. One must observe such things if one wants to know what the earth once looked like.

Today, however, things are done in quite a different way, and in order that your judgement of what I am telling you here may not be confused by what is commonly accepted, I would like to give you a small view of this general knowledge. It agrees perfectly with what I say if only one considers it in the right way.

People today do not think about things as we have done here in the last two lectures. They say: Here is the earth; it is made of mineral substance. This mineral earth is convenient to investigate, so let us examine first what lies on top, what we walk on. Then if we make quarries, if we make railway cuttings and open up the ground, we find there are certain layers or strata of earth. The uppermost layer is the one on which we walk. If we dig deeper somewhere or other, we find deeper-lying strata. But these strata are not always lying so nicely above one another that we can say: the one is always on top of the other.

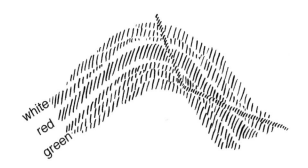

When you really examine the earth, here you have one stratum [see drawing—red], it is curved over, not level; another stratum below is also curved [green]. And above them comes the stratum on which we walk [white]. Now, as long as we remain on foot on this side of a hill we find an upper layer that could become good arable land if we would use the right manuring methods and so on. But if we are building a railway we may have to remove certain strata and by making these cuttings we delve further into the earth. That has led to the discovery that strata are superimposed on one another, not level, but they have been jumbled up in all sorts of ways.

But these strata are sometimes very remarkable. People have asked how one can determine the age of the strata — which layer is older. Of course the most obvious answer is this: when the strata lie above one another, then the lowest is the oldest, the next above younger, and the one closest to the surface the youngest of all. But, you see, that is not always the case. In some places it is so, but not everywhere. And one can show in the following way why it is not the case everywhere.

We are accustomed, as you know, in our civilized lands to bury our domestic animals when they die, so that they may not be injurious to people. But if the human race were not so far evolved, what would happen with the animals then? Wherever the animal died, there it would lie. Now at first it would remain on the surface. But, as you know, when it rains the soil gets washed up and after a time part of the decaying creature would be mingled with the soil thrown up by the rain. There it would remain, and after some time the whole animal would be penetrated with earth by the rain or by water that flows down over a slope, and then eventually the whole animal would be covered in earth. Now someone can come along and say: 'Heavens! The earth looks so uneven there, I must dig and have a look!' He need not dig very far, just a little, and then he finds what is left of the skeleton, let us say, of a wild horse. Then he says: 'Well, now I'm walking on a stratum that only appeared later. The one below was formed when there were wild horses like that.' And one can know that that is the next stratum, that the age in which this man lives was preceded by an age in which these horses lived.

You see, what that man does is what the geologists have been doing with all the strata of the earth, ever since the time when they could be reached by quarries, railway cuttings, excavations, and so on. One learns in geology to investigate quarries everywhere, with a hammer or some other instrument, in order to record what is exposed in the mountains through landslides or something similar. One goes hammering everywhere, makes various statements and then one finds in some stratum the so-called fossils. Then one can say that there are strata beneath the ground that contain animals quite different from those of today. Then one discovers in excavating the earth's strata what the animals were like that existed in other ages.

This is nothing so very special, for people often underestimate the time it takes for something like this to happen. People find today in southern regions churches or other buildings just standing there. The people come along, do some digging for some reason or other, and — good heavens! There's something under this church that is hard; that's not earth. They dig down and find a pagan temple underneath! What had happened? A relatively short time ago this surface layer on which the church or building stands was not there at all. It was deposited by man, perhaps with the help of natural forces, and underneath there is the pagan temple. What was once above is now below. Layer upon layer has in fact been piled up in the earth. And one must find out, not from the way the strata lie, but from the nature of the fossils, how these animals and the various plants have come into the strata.

Then, however, the following comes about. You find one layer of the earth [see drawing on page 36, yellow], you find another [green]; you are able for some reason or other to excavate [arrow], and if you look merely at the stratification, then it seems as if what I have marked green were the lower layer and what I have marked yellow were the upper

green

yellow

layer. You cannot get in here at all, you cannot excavate, there is no railway, no tunnel or anything else by which one can get in. You make a note that the yellow is the upper stratum, the green the lower. But you must not decide immediately, you must first look for fossils.

Now one very frequently finds fossils in the *upper* stratum which are earlier—of fish, for example, strange fish-skeletons which are from an earlier period. And perhaps below one finds interesting mammal skeletons which are more recent. Now the fossils contradict the strata; up above appear the older (the earlier), below, the more recent (the younger). One must realize how that has happened. You see, it is because some sort of earthquake, some inner movement has flung what was below up over the top layer. It is the same as if I were to lay a chair on the table so that its original position was here the chair-back and there the table-top; and then through an earthquake the table was flung over the chair.

One can perceive in the most varied instances that there has been an inversion, a turning upside down. And one can come to the following conclusion as to when the inversion took place: it must have happened after all the fossils were formed, otherwise they would lie differently.

One comes in this way not to judge the strata simply as they lie one above the other, but one must be able to see how they have changed their positions. The Alps, this mighty chain of mountains stretching from the Mediterranean to the Danube region, this main mountain range in Switzerland, is not to be understood at all unless one can go into such things. For all the strata that were built up in the Alps have later been thoroughly jumbled up. There what was lowest often lies at the top, and what was at the top is lowest of all. One must first find out how all these shifts have taken place.

It is only when all this is taken into account that one can tell which are the oldest strata and which are the newest. Modern science, only undertaking external research, naturally says: Those strata are the oldest in which the remains of the very simplest animals and plants are found. Later on, animals and plants grew more complicated, and so we find the most complicated remains in the latest strata. In the oldest strata one finds fossils because the calcium or quartz structure of the animal has been preserved, while everything else has been dissolved. When one comes to the later strata the skeleton has been preserved.

Now there is another remarkable way in which fossils are formed. Sometimes this is very interesting. Imagine some simple type of ancient creature; it might have had tentacles in front. I am drawing it rather large; in the strata known to geology it will as a rule be smaller. Now this creature perishes as it lies on this piece of ground, and this particular soil does not penetrate and permeate the creature; it avoids, so to say, the acids in the body. Then something very remarkable occurs: the earth in which the animal lies approaches it from all sides and envelops it, and a hollow space is made in the shape of the animal. That has happened very frequently; such hollow spaces are formed, earth is shaped around the animal. But there is nothing inside; the soil has not been absorbed by the body, but surrounds and envelops the animal and so a hollow space is formed. Later, the animal's scales are dissolved and still

white

later a brook winds through. This then fills the hollow space with stony substance [green], and there, within, a cast of the animal is finely modelled, by a quite different material. Such casts are particularly interesting, for there we don't have the animals themselves, but their casts.

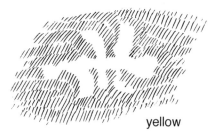

yellow

However, you must not imagine that things are always so easy. Of present man, for instance, with his organism of soft substance, there is extraordinarily little left — nor of the higher animals. There are animals of which only the casts of their teeth have remained. One finds casts of the teeth of a kind of primeval shark which were formed in this way. One

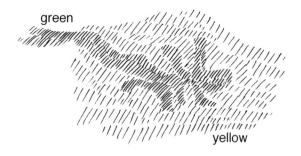

green

yellow

comes to realize that every animal has its own form of teeth and man has a different form. The dental formation is always in keeping with the whole structure of the creature. One must have the talent to imagine the appearance of the whole animal from the form of its teeth. So things are by no means simple.

But as one studies these strata one finds out how things really developed. And then it simply becomes clear that there was a time when such animals as we have now did not exist, when there were much, much simpler creatures, somewhat like our snails, mussels, and so on. But one has to know how much has remained of them. Let us imagine that the following could happen. Just suppose that a small boy who did not like to eat crab sneaked a crab from his parents' dinner-table and played with it. He is not caught, and buries it in the garden. Now there is earth over it and the whole business is forgotten. Later the garden belongs to new owners; they dig about and in one place they see two funny little things looking like lime-shells. (You know about the crab's so-called eyes which are not eyes, but little shells of calcium in the body of the crab.) Those are the only traces left.

Now one cannot say that those are fossils of some kind of animal; they are fossils of only part of the creature. Similarly in older strata, especially in the Alps, one finds some sort of fossil having that shell-like appearance. That is how they look; they no longer exist today but are found in the earlier strata. One must not suppose, however, that this had been the whole creature. One must assume that there was something around it that dissolved, and only a small piece of the animal is left.

Modern science goes into this very little. Why? Well, it simply says that in this mighty Alpine mass the layers have been mixed with one another, the lowest flung to the top, the uppermost to the lowest — that the strata show it. But can you imagine, gentlemen, that with the present earth-forces such massive mountains could be flung up in that way? The little bit of movement that happens now on earth is by comparison a gentle dance of one fleck lightly tossed on another — today that is all, a sort of slight permeation!

If someone lived 720 years instead of 72, he would find in his old age that he was walking on ground a little higher than it had originally been. But we live too short a life. Just think if a fly that only lives from morning till evening were to relate what it experiences! Since it lives only in the summer, it would tell us of nothing but flowers, that there were always flowers. It would have no idea of what goes on in the winter; it would believe that each summer followed the one before. We human beings are certainly a little longer-lived than a one-day fly, but still we have a little of the fly nature with our 70 to 72 years! We see indeed little of what goes on. Even with the scanty forces prevailing today in the earth, there is no doubt that more happens than people usually see. Yet comparatively speaking all that happens is that rivers flow to the sea and leave alluvial soil behind. So a little soil is deposited, and this then reaches beyond the banks and the fields get a new stratum. That is comparatively little. When one considers how something like this great mountain mass of the Alps has been jolted and shaken through and through, it is obvious that the forces which are active today were active in a quite different way in earlier times.

But now we must try to picture how such a thing can happen. Take, for instance, an egg cell from some mammal. It looks at first quite simple, a nucleus in the centre with an albuminous mass all around. Now suppose that the egg is fertilized. When it is fertilized, the nucleus changes into all sorts of little forms; it develops very strangely into a number of spirals that go up like tails. And then the moment these little coils arise, star-formed structures develop out of the mass. The whole mass starts forming and becoming structured because there is life in it. What goes on there is very different from what goes on in our earth today. The upheavals and overturnings that are taking place in the egg cell are the same as what once took place in the massive Alps!

So there is nothing more natural than to deduce that the earth must once have been alive, or these convulsions of inverting and overthrusting could not possibly have occurred! The present form of the earth does in fact show us that in past ages when neither man nor higher animal existed, the earth itself was alive. This obliges us to say that the present dead earth has come forth from a living earth. Yet animals can only live on this present dead earth! Just think, if the oxygen and nitrogen in the air had not separated off and had not condemned hydrogen, carbon and sulphur to relative passivity, we would then have to breathe in something like egg-white—for that was what surrounded the earth.

Now we could imagine—for anything is possible—that instead of our lungs, we had developed organs able to draw in an albuminous atmosphere like that. Today, of course, we can take it in as food through the mouth. Why couldn't a sort of lung-organ have evolved, closer to the mouth? Anything can originate in this world; any possible thing might come about—even though we would never guess at such changes from observing man's present body. But think, gentlemen—nowadays we look out into lifeless air. It has died. Formerly the albumen was living. The air has died because the sulphur, hydrogen and carbon have gone and the nitrogen and oxygen have therefore also perished. We gaze into light-filled air that has died, but this has allowed our eyes to be physical, as they are indeed physical. If everything in our surroundings were living, then our eyes would have to be living too. But if they were living, we would be unable to see with them, and we would always be in a state of unconsciousness — just as a person becomes unconscious when there begins to be too much life in his head, when instead of the regularly developed organs he has all sorts of growths. He is then unconscious intermittently, and later it becomes so severe that he lies there as if he were dead. Likewise in our original condition on the earth, as it was then, we could not have lived consciously. The human being could only awake to consciousness as the earth gradually died. And so mankind evolves on an earth that is dead.

So it is, gentlemen! And this is true not only of nature but also of civilization. If you think back to what I said just now — that below the earth there could be pagan temples and above Christian churches — you will see that the Christian churches are related to the pagan temples just as the upper strata to the lower, only that in one case we have to do with nature, in the other with culture. But one will not understand how the Christian element evolved if one does not observe that it evolved out of paganism as its foundation. In culture too we have to consider these strata.

Now I have said that the human being has actually been there all the time, but as a spiritual being, not a physical being. And that again leads us to look for the real reason why man did not evolve as a physical being sooner. We have said that in the air today there are nitrogen and oxygen, with carbon, hydrogen and sulphur to a lesser degree. In our breathing we ourselves unite the carbon that is in us with the oxygen we inhale, and exhale the two together as carbon dioxide. In our human existence we breathe in oxygen and breathe out carbon dioxide; our life consists of that. We would long, long ago have filled the earth and the air of the earth with carbon dioxide had there not been something else on the earth: the plants. They have the same hunger for carbon that we have for oxygen. They take up the carbon dioxide eagerly, hold on to the carbon and give out the oxygen again.

You see, gentlemen, how wonderfully these things complement each other! We human beings need the oxygen from the air, we inhale it, unite it with the carbon we have within us and exhale carbon and oxygen together as carbon dioxide. The plants breathe this in and breathe the oxygen out again, and so there is always oxygen in the air.

Well, this is true today but in human evolution on the earth it was not always like that. When we find the fossilized creatures that lived long ago, we realize that they could not have been like our modern animals and plants, particularly not like our present plants. All the primeval plants must have been much more like our sponges, mushrooms, algae. There is a difference between our mushrooms and our other present plants. The latter take in the carbon and form their body from it. When they sink into the ground, their body remains as coal. The coal we mine today is the remains of plants.

All the research we are able to pursue into the kinds of plants that originally existed tells us the following. Our present plants, including the plants which now provide us with coal, are built up from carbon. But much earlier plants were formed not from carbon but from nitrogen. That was possible because, just as carbon dioxide is exhaled today by animal and man, in ancient times a combination of carbon and nitrogen was exhaled. That is prussic acid, the terribly poisonous hydrocyanic acid fatal to all life today. This poisonous prussic acid was once exhaled, and nothing that exists today could then have arisen. The early mushroom-like plants took in the nitrogen and formed their body from it. The creatures about which I spoke last time, the birdlike beings and the heavy, coarse animal-beings, breathed out this poisonous acid, and the plants around them took the nitrogen to form their plant-body. Here, too, we can see that substances still existing today were used in quite a different way in ancient times.

I spoke of this once before to those of you who have been here for some time. I related how in 1906 I had to give some lectures in Paris[4] on the evolution of the earth, the origin of man, and so forth. The subject led me to ask whether anything in this world can show that carbon and oxygen have not always had the role they play today, that nitrogen once had that role, and that once the atmosphere consisted of prussic acid, of hydrocyanic acid.

Now you know that there are old people and young children. Well, if a man of 70 stands here and a child of two next to him, they are both human beings; they stand beside each other, and the one who is now 70 was like the two-year-old 68 years ago. Things of different ages stand side by side. And it is the same in the universe; there, too, the older and the younger are side by side. Our earth, from what I have just now described and what you can still see today, our earth is a greybeard, an ancient fellow, almost dead already — if one does not count newly springing life, one can call it almost dead. But by its side in the universe there are also younger forms which will only later become what our present life is. For instance, we must regard the comets as one of these forms. We can know, therefore, that since the comets are younger, they must still have conditions that belong to a younger age. The comets are to the earth what the child is to the old man. And if the earth once had prussic acid, the comets must now have it, they must have hydro-cyanic acid! If with today's body one were to touch a comet, one would instantly die, for they contain diluted prussic acid.

I said in Paris in 1906 that this follows from the premises of spiritual science. Those who acknowledge spiritual science accepted my statement even though it astonished them. Then later, a fairly long time afterwards, a comet made its appearance. By that time people had got the necessary instruments and it was then found by ordinary scientific methods that comets do have cyanide, prussic acid, as I had said in Paris in 1906. So it was confirmed.

Naturally, when people hear of this, they call it a coincidence: Oh sure, Steiner made that statement in Paris, and then there was the discovery — just a coincidence. They say this because they know nothing else. But I have now told you why one must take it for granted that there is prussic acid in comets. It was no accident, it was genuine science by which one first arrived at this knowledge. Physical research only confirmed it later. People realize now that this is true for all that anthroposophy describes; for everything is confirmed later. In our times quite a number of things will be discovered outside the anthroposophical movement that were already presented many years ago by anthroposophy in a rather different way.

Yes, there are many other things that could be carefully investigated today by science. I often say that if people could really travel to a star they would be amazed to find it different from modern ideas about it that arise from earthly conceptions. They imagine that a star contains a glowing gas. But that is not at all what is found out there. Actually, where the star is there is empty space, empty space that would immediately suck one up. Suction forces are there. They would suck you up instantly, split you to pieces. If people would work with the same consistent research and the same unprejudiced thinking as we do here, they would also come to see with intricate spectroscopes that there are not gases out there, but negative suctional space.

Some time ago I gave certain individuals the task of investigating the sun and stars with the spectroscope, simply in order to prove by external methods that the stars are hollow spaces, not glowing gases. That can be proved. The persons to whom I gave this task were tremendously enthusiastic when they started: 'Oh now we shall get somewhere!' But sometimes enthusiasm fades away; they delayed too long. And then a year-and-a-half ago news came from America that people were starting to investigate the stars and were gradually finding out that they were not glowing gases but empty space, a vacuum! It is no disaster, of course, for such a thing to happen. But naturally, it would have been more useful to us—in an outward sense—if we had done it. But it doesn't matter, as long as truth comes to light.

On the other hand, however, it can be seen through just such things that anthroposophy really wants to work in collaboration with ordinary science. So it would also like to work with ordinary science on the strata of the earth. One thoroughly accepts what science has to say about the upheavals and overturnings in the Alps. But one cannot go along with the scientists when they assume that these upheavals were caused by forces that still exist today. The fact is that there were *life-forces* there then; only life-forces could have flung and tossed these strata of living substance through one another. Anthroposophy incorporates ordinary science and then goes far beyond it, but science always wants to stop whenever it is too lazy to examine things more closely.

So—we will continue on Wednesday at nine o'clock.

The origins of the world and the human being— Lemuria and Atlantis

Rudolf Steiner: Good morning, gentlemen! Perhaps today we can finish what we began last time.

I explained to you that we must form a mental picture of how the earth has gradually evolved and how the human being was always present spiritually. Physically — that is, in a body — man first appeared, as we have seen, when the earth had become dead, when the earth itself had lost its vitality. As I told you last time, it was only a short while ago that people thought of the earth in such a way that they looked for the fossils in it in order to determine the age of its strata. Conceptions such as are now held by science have been formed only comparatively recently, and we have seen to what an extent these conceptions are actually false and cannot stand up in face of the facts.

Now you must realize that when people dig and burrow into the earth as I described to you, when they examine something like the Alpine range with its jumbled strata, they then find quite distinct fossilized plants and animals in every single layer. And the plants and animals that fill the earth today have appeared only recently. Earlier plant and animal forms were different from the plants and animals of the present day.

That the earth has not evolved simply and gradually, with one stratum slowly piling up over another until the earth was finally formed, can be seen not only from the fact that the Alps are jumbled together but also from the following. There were once animals similar to our elephants but larger. Our elephant is certainly large enough, but these animals were still more powerful, with still thicker skins. Still heavier pachyderms once lived. This is acknowledged because they have been found in northern Siberia where Russia stretches over into Asia. All these remarkable animals, these mammoths, have been found as complete animals with their flesh in perfect condition.

You see, one can keep the flesh of animals well preserved if one puts them into ice. And these animals were actually in ice! These animals lived near the Arctic Ocean where Siberia approaches the North Pole; they are still there today, as fresh as if they had been caught yesterday by giants and put in ice to be preserved! Yet such animals do not live today, these are primeval animals. Also they cannot possibly have perished slowly for they are preserved as complete animals. The only explanation can be that when they were alive a mighty water catastrophe suddenly occurred, and this water froze in the region of the North Pole, immediately overwhelming them.

We see from this that in earlier times there were quite extraordinary happenings on the earth which cannot be compared to the situation today. And if we look at the Alps, we have to think that these events cannot have gone on through millions of years but must have taken place in a comparatively short time—that everything in the earth must have bubbled up and been alive as it is in one's stomach after one has eaten and begins to digest. But that can only take place in something living. The earth must have been living. And the forces that were in the earth have been left behind. In those times there were large, heavy animals. Our slighter, more supple animals were formed after the earth itself had died and was itself no longer a living being. These large elephants, these mammoths, were, so to speak, like lice on the old body of the earth and were destroyed by a single wave that turned to ice.

You can understand how well this agrees with what I

have said about our present earth being a kind of world-corpse. And the human being could develop only when recent conditions came about on the earth.

I would now like to speak of something that will show you how the earth has altered — and altered comparatively recently. If we think of the earth, on the one hand we have America; on the other hand we have Europe: Norway, Scotland, England, Ireland, and also France and Spain, and Italy and Germany, as far as the Baltic Sea. Now if we travel today, let us say, from Liverpool to America, we travel over the Atlantic Ocean. Now I want to tell you something. On this side (Africa is down below) certain plants and certain animals are found everywhere (and, of course, we must include small animal life). If today we look at the plants and animals living on the western coasts of Europe and Africa, and then look at the other side, the eastern coast of America, we discover that these plants and animals are in some way related to one another. They are different, but they are related. Why? Well, it is like this. Down below is the floor of the ocean, above is the water of the Atlantic, then here is Africa. How the plants and animals came to be here and how they came to be there can only be explained if once there was land here everywhere, high land, where the animals could cross over and the plants scatter their seeds, not over an ocean, but over land. Thus where today there is an immense sea, an immense ocean, between Europe and America, there was once land. The ground has sunk. Wherever ground sinks water appears immediately. If you dig down to a certain depth anywhere in the earth, water immediately appears.

So we must assume that the land there has sunk. For instance, this is interesting: here is Italy, here is Ravenna — now if one walks from the city of Ravenna to the sea it takes more than an hour, but while walking from Ravenna to the sea one finds mussels and sea shells everywhere on the ground. That is proof that the sea was once there. And Ravenna, now an hour from the sea, was once right on it! — the sea bordered it. But there the land rose, was raised up, and the water flowed away from it. If land is raised especially high, it becomes desolate; then it becomes cold, as happens in the mountains. One such region that has become cold is the region of Siberia. Siberia shows through all its plant growth and so forth that at one time its land was much lower, that it has risen tremendously.

And so you can see the land continually rises and sinks in certain parts of the earth. It rises … sinks … and we see that land and water on the earth are distributed at different times in the most varied ways. If one looks at the rocks of the British Isles, of England, Scotland and Ireland, looking at the layers themselves one finds that England has risen and sunk four times in the course of its existence! When it was above, certain plants grew until it sank. Naturally when it rose again, it was barren waste. It covered itself with quite different plants and animals, and today one can discover that it has risen and sunk four times.

Thus the earth is in continual movement. In very ancient times it was much greater, much more powerful movement. If today everything were in movement as it was in those times, it would be really unpleasant for mankind. The last accounts of mighty earth movements are those of the Flood, and they have come down to humanity only in legendary form. But the Flood was only a small matter compared with the gigantic upheavals that once took place on the earth.

Therefore, gentlemen, the question surely arises: How did human beings ever arrive on this earth at all? How did man ever appear? And as to that, there have been the most diverse ideas. The most convenient opinion people have formed is this, that there were once apelike animals which gradually perfected themselves and became human beings. That is the view science held in the nineteenth century. It no longer holds that view; but the general public, who always straggle along after science, still, of course, believe it. Now how could anyone imagine that the human being, physical man as he now is on the physical earth, could have fashioned himself? There was, so to speak, a great rumpus and tremendous enthusiasm when at the end of the nineteenth century a learned traveller, Dubois,[5] discovered parts of a skeleton in East Asia, in strata of the earth where up to that time it had been thought that man could not have lived. There were parts of a skeleton believed to be a human skeleton: the upper part of a thigh, a few teeth and pieces of the upper part of a skull. That is what Dubois found over there in Asia. Such a thing must, of course, have a suitable name, so he called these remains *Pithecanthropus erectus*.

People had the idea that this creature was representative of an apelike species from which mankind then gradually evolved. And then people developed various ideas of how man did evolve in this way. Some say that an apelike race lived in conditions that forced it to work, and so the feet, the apelike climbing feet, were transformed into straight feet, and the climbing forefeet into human hands ... and so it changed completely. On the other hand, others object and say: 'No, that cannot be, for if this ape-man had come into such unfavourable conditions, he would simply have died, then he could not have transformed himself. So this ape-man must have lived in a kind of paradise where he was able to maintain himself and develop quite freely, where he was protected.' You see how far apart the views are! But none of this holds good when we undertake a real examination of the facts of which we have spoken.

Let us go back to them again. There was once a large expanse of land where today there is the Atlantic Ocean over which one travels when going from Europe to America — large areas of land. But you see, if we investigate the fossils found here under the earth, and from them deduce what the earlier forms and species were—of both plants and animals—we discover that it cannot have been like this there! The earth between our present Europe and America must have been much softer, not solid mineral as it is today, and the air must have been much denser, always misty, containing much water and other substances. Thus there was much softer ground and much denser air. In such a region, if today there could be one on earth, we could not live for a week, we would die at once. But as it cannot have been so very long ago, 10,000 to 15,000 years, human beings must, of course, have lived at that time. So they cannot have been like today's human beings.

Present-day man has his solid bone structure only because there are hard minerals in the world outside. To our calcareous bones belong also the calcareous mountains with which we continually exchange calcium; we drink it in our water, and so forth. In that earlier time there was not yet such a solid bony skeleton. Human beings could have had only soft cartilage, like sharks. Also they could not have breathed through lungs as we do today. At that time they had to have a kind of swimming bladder and a kind of gills, so that the human being who lived then was in his external form half man and half fish. We cannot escape the fact that man then looked quite different—half man and half fish. And if we go back to still earlier times we find that man was much, much softer. If we go still further back he was watery, quite fluid. So naturally no fossils were formed then; man was just absorbed into the rest of the earth's fluids. So that is the way we have grown into what we are today. When we are still in our mother's womb, we are a little bag of fluid. But that is something very small. In those times we were huge, great fluid or jelly-like beings. And the further we go back in Earth evolution, the more liquid man becomes and the more he is really a soft jelly-like mass—not formed out of present-day water, for out of that, naturally, no man could be made—but out of a substance somewhat like albumen. Out of such a substance it was possible for the human being to be formed.

So we go back to an age when there was neither the present human form nor the present elephants, nor rhinoceroses, nor lions, nor cows, nor oxen, nor bulls, nor kangaroos—none of these were yet there. On the other hand we can say there were fishlike creatures—not like present-day fish, but already manlike—beings half human, half fish, that one could, after all, call man. There were all these. But there were still none of the animal forms of today.

Then the earth gradually changed into the form it has today. The floor of the Atlantic Ocean sank ever more and more; the boggy, slimy, albumen-like condition gradually changed into the present water and gradually brought about a change in these fish-men. But the most diverse forms arose. The more imperfect of these fish-men became kangaroos, those a little more advanced became deer and cattle, and the most perfect became apes or men. You see from this that man did not descend from apes; man was there, and all the mammals really descended from him, from these human forms in which man remained imperfect. So we must say that the ape descended from man, not that man descended from the ape. That is so, and we must be quite clear about it.

You see, you could make it clear to yourselves through the following. Imagine a really clever man who has a small son. This son suffers from hydrocephalus and is very dull-witted. Let us say that the clever man is about 45 and the small son seven or eight. The boy turns out to be dull-witted. Now could anyone say that because the boy is a small, imperfect human being, the mature man, the clever, perfect person is descended from the small, imperfect person? It would be nonsense! The fact is that the small, imperfect being is descended from the clever one; the other assertion would be a mistake. This mistake was made when it was thought that apes, the manlike beings who were left behind, are man's ancestors. They are the human beings left behind, so to speak, the imperfect specimens of mankind left behind. We might say that in this matter science pursued a path that led it deep into error while less learned people had more sense. We need only remember the story of the small schoolboy. His teacher, caught up in a modern scientific outlook, announced: 'Men are descended from monkeys.' The boy came home with this piece of wisdom. His father said: 'You silly! Perhaps you did, but I didn't!' You see, there you have the naïve man versus Darwinism. Science is often not as clever as a naïve person. We must acknowledge that.

And so we may say: All that lives out in the world as animal is descended from the primeval being that was neither animal nor man but something between. The one remained imperfect, the other became more perfect, became the human being. Of course now people come along and say: 'Yes, but earlier human beings were far less perfect than they are today; in earlier times they had a skull with a lower forehead, a nose like this—Neanderthal man, or the human remains found in Yugoslavia.' (These are seldom found and we must not think that such skeletons lie around everywhere; only a few have been found.) Contemporary man usually has a lofty forehead and looks different. So people say: 'Those primitive people with the low foreheads were naturally stupid, for the forehead is the seat of the intellect, and only people who develop high foreheads have proper intelligence—therefore primitive people were without intelligence, and of course those who came later with prominent foreheads had a proper mind.'

You see, if we had looked at the people of Atlantis, those who lived before the floor of the Atlantic Ocean sank and the sea rose, we would have found that they had quite a thin skin, a little soft cartilage—like a net—as covering for the head; and all the rest of them was water. If you look today at someone with hydrocephalus, he does not have a backward sloping forehead, but a high, prominent one, so the Atlantean head was much more like the hydrocephalic head. Imagine that the Atlantean had this head, but watery, such as we see today in an embryo. Think of the earth and of how the ground sank where the Atlantic Ocean is now, and thus the Atlantic Ocean came into being. Europe and Asia rose more and more; there everything rose. In America the earth rose also, while in between it sank. The earth changed. Human beings acquired harder bones. So when we go back into earlier times when the area of the Atlantic Ocean was still solid land, people had soft bones, just cartilage; there was still water in them. And human beings could also think with the water. Now you will say: For heaven's sake! Now he expects us to believe that people of that time did their thinking not with a solid brain, but a watery one! But indeed, gentlemen, none of you think with your solid brain! You all think with the water in which your brain floats; it is superstitious to imagine that you think with your solid brain. Not even the obstinate thickheads who can grasp nothing but the ideas which they accepted in early youth— not even they think with their solid brain; they also think with the brain water, although with the denser parts of it!

But then came the time when this kind of water, this slimy, albuminous water, disappeared. People could no longer think with it; the bones remained, and that low skull appeared. It was only later—in Europe and over in America—that this grew out again to a high forehead. So we must say, the old Atlanteans had very high foreheads in their watery heads. Then, as I said, when the water disappeared, low foreheads appeared at first, and then they gradually grew out again into high foreheads. It was just in a transitional age that people looked like Neanderthal man, or like the remains found in the south of France or in Sicily. They were a transitional human being who lived in the coast areas where the ground gradually sank. The humans we dig up today in the south of France are not primitive people but later human beings. They are our ancestors, but of a later period.

And it is interesting that, belonging to the same period in which these human beings with a flat, low forehead must have lived, we find caves where there are things which tell us that the people of that time did not live in houses, but in places in the earth where they dug themselves in. But for that the earth must first have become hard. So at the time when the earth was not yet quite so hard as it is today, or at least somewhat less hard, people burrowed into the earth to make their dwelling-places, and these we still find today. And the most remarkable things we find in them are paintings and drawings, which are comparatively simple but which reproduce quite skilfully animals living at that time. Today people are really astonished that those people with flat foreheads, with undeveloped heads, could have made those drawings. The drawings are clever in one respect and crude in another. How can we explain this? It is because people had once lived with high, still fluid foreheads and had already had art; perhaps they were able to do much more than we can; this art then atrophied. And what we find in the caves are just the last remnants of what people were still able to do. So we can see that once human beings did not live merely as animals, gradually perfecting themselves to their present condition, but that before the present human race was here on earth with its solid bones, there was another human race with more cartilage, a race that already possessed a high culture and civilization.

I have told you that birds were also different in ancient times from what they are now. Birds once consisted entirely of air; later, they built a body around this. Hence their bones are filled with air. The birds were once creatures consisting only of air, but of dense air. And the present birds formed their feathers and so on when our kind of air originated. Just think, if our birds had schools and a culture (they do not, of course, have them, but we can use our imagination), these would have to look different from ours! Take, for instance, the houses we build. These constitute a large part of our civilization. But birds can't build houses—they would fall down; neither can birds become sculptors. They can't even use needle and thread—that also belongs to civilization. If birds had a civilization and a culture, what would it be like? It would have to be above in the air. But it could not include anything solid; they couldn't have a writing desk, or anything else. At most, they could make signs that would be gone the moment they made them. But if the others understood the signs—well, that would be a culture.

Now imagine an eagle that was a very clever creature, an eagle able to make a statue of an owl—yet he would have to make it in the air only; nothing of it would be there if one looked for it. Now supposing the owl came—a particularly vain owl—and ordered the eagle to make an owl-statue of itself. He would make it very beautifully, very beautifully. Perhaps he would make it just when there was a little cloud, so that he had some denser air—even so, it would disappear at once. Other birds could fly to see it, other owls also, and admire it. Birds can't do that today! You may be quite certain that the eagle will not make a statue of an owl! But the beings who were once people with a soft structure, soft bodies, had a culture and civilization like that. When, for instance, there was land where the Atlantic Ocean is now, then things could be more or less firm, although the land always sank again, but it was already denser. This was preceded by a less dense condition when there was only a culture and civilization that people made in signs that disappeared at once. So we must imagine that these human beings shaped everything once upon a time, but nothing lasted; it was there in very delicate matter. And when later they began to shape things that were more coarse, these were clumsy. Even today it is easier to shape something in soft wax than in harder clay. And when human beings had their whole culture and civilization in only a sort of dense air, they had joy in making something even if it vanished at once.

But now, gentlemen, you can see that we have gone very far back into the past and have found human beings who really consisted only of dense air. Imagine it like this. There is a person of dense air, who has the appearance of a cloud, only not so irregularly formed, for he has what definitely looks like a face, a head and limbs. But it is something very spiritual; it is almost a ghost! If you met something like it today, you would take it for a ghost, and indeed a very peculiar ghost. It would look somewhat like a fish—and then again somewhat like a human being. We were once like that. So now we have already arrived back at a stage when human beings were really quite spiritual. And the further back we go, the more we find that man as spirit dominates matter. We present human beings can do this only with the softest elements of matter. If we take a piece of bread into our mouth, we can bite it and make it liquid—for all food has to become liquid if it is to pass into the human body. Just think! You make bread liquid; it goes into the oesophagus, into the stomach, spreads out into the blood. What really becomes of that piece of bread? Now that is a remarkable story.

Suppose you have a person before you, the human form, with stomach and oesophagus, leading to the mouth. Now the person eats a piece of bread. He takes it into his mouth; there it gradually becomes liquid; here in the stomach it is made still more liquid, now it spreads out into the blood, it goes everywhere, becomes thin, thinner, and is dispersed.

And so I have a piece of bread in my hand. I eat it; after a while what does it look like? After three hours when it has spread out into the blood, into the whole body, it is like this: that piece of bread has itself become a person. Thus everything you eat as food is transformed into a human being, only you do not notice it. You do not notice that really everything you take into yourself continually becomes yourself. You could not be a human being if you did not continually make yourself anew. For what you eat today, on the ninth of July, becomes an extremely rarefied human being; something of it remains, the rest passes away. And so it is the next day, and the next; in this way your body is renewed. Every seven years it is completely renewed.

Gentlemen, today we need this solid body so that we can continually remake our human being. But earlier people did not have this solid body. They could do this out of their souls; what they took in they could so shape that it looked like the human being of that time. You have to imagine that they had no need of muscles and bones, but by means of the soul they could so transform their food that it became human-like. So it was, truly. Man through his spirit governed matter, substance, and shaped his own form, although it was much more delicate. But there he was: a manlike hovering cloud. This form is still in us today, but we have a frame for it: bones and muscles. These must be there as the frame. And in reality when we take food, we still today make this human form. Once upon a time man was as tenuous, as rarefied as the form we create in ourselves today when we eat.

We also breathe air. First it is outside; then it is in us. And the air too spreads out everywhere through our blood. A person of air is formed today throughout the entire human being. The person of air comes into being. So if I tell you that man was once aeriform before he became densified and

crystallized through his bones, I am not telling you something that does not still occur today. Every time you take a
breath you still form this person of air. In earlier times this
alone existed; only later were our solid, thick, earthly parts
built in. So we come back to the fact that what we see today
as firm, solid matter was once spiritual through and
through. Therefore it is nonsense to say that once the earth
consisted only of gas, and that this gas through its own
forces formed itself into the human beings and animals of
today. Instead we can see that human beings and animals
and everything existing now were themselves once gaseous
and aeriform and have undergone a metamorphosis.

So we find a condition of our earth that must once have
been like this: an area of land where water is today. Where
we now travel over water there was once land. At that time
the land that is now Europe was deeply submerged; it rose
only later; only in isolated places was it above the surface.
Now we come to Europe. There we now have ground that
earlier was deeply submerged, the top of which was
covered with boggy water. We come to Asia, which was
completely covered with swamps. Over in America there
were also swamps. Those regions which today are solid
earth were then sea, and where there is sea today there was
land. The human beings who lived there looked quite different from present-day man; they were thin, delicate. Only
when the present lands rose out of the water and the earlier
lands sank and became sea—only then did the present
human race appear and the present-day animals in the form
they now bear. This is connected with the inner life of the
earth.

Today it all happens more subtly. Today the lands no
longer rise and sink so violently, but they still continue to
rise and sink slightly. Anyone who at the present time
studies maps—even of Switzerland—maps which are only
a few centuries old, sees a lake somewhere and today some

place may be quite far from that lake, but we know that just as Ravenna was once on the sea, so this place must once have been on the lake. Lakes dry up and become smaller, even today — only the process is slower than it used to be. But because the land surfaces and the sea floors rise and fall, human beings and animals are continually changing, continually transforming. But this proceeds more slowly than it used to do.

That is what I wanted to tell you. You see now how the present human race has developed. Next time we will add something historical, because once the human race was on earth in its present form, history began. Only when they were obliged to be hunters, farmers, shepherds did human beings develop history. That is where we can still add a piece of history to what we have been able to say today about the origin of the world and man. It is good that Herr Dollinger raised the question. We have been able to speak about it in detail and, as I have said, next time we will add a little history.

Origin and particular character of Chinese and Indian cultures

Rudolf Steiner: Gentlemen! I mentioned our wish to look further into the history that is connected with our present study of the world. You have seen how the human race gradually built itself up out of the rest of nature. It was only when conditions on the earth were such that human beings were able to live upon it—when the earth had died, when it no longer had its own life—that human and animal life could develop in the way I have described.

Now we have also seen that in the beginning human life was actually quite different from what it is today, and unfolded where the Atlantic Ocean is now. We have to imagine that where the Atlantic Ocean is today, there was formerly solid ground. Today we have Asia on the one hand, the Black Sea here, below it Africa, then Russia and Asia itself. On the other hand, there is England, Ireland, and over there also America. Formerly everything in between was land, and here very little land; over here in Europe at that time there was actually a really huge sea. These countries were all in the sea, and when we come up to the north, Siberia was sea too; it was still all sea. Below where India is today, the land rose a little above the sea. Thus we actually have some land there, and land on this side too. Where today we find the Asian peoples, the inhabitants of the Near East and those of Europe, there was sea—the land only rising up later. The land, however, went much farther, continuing right on to the Pacific Ocean where today there are so many islands, Java, Sumatra, and so on; they were all part of the continent that used to be there—all this archipelago. Thus, where the Pacific Ocean now is there was a great deal of land with sea between the two land masses.

Now the first peoples we are able to investigate remained in this region, here, where the land was preserved. When we look around us in Europe we can really say: ten, twelve or fifteen thousand years ago the earth, the ground, became sufficiently firm for human beings to dwell upon it. Before that, only marine animals were there which developed out of the sea, and so on. If at that time you had looked for man, he would have been where the Atlantic Ocean is today. But over there in Asia, in eastern Asia, there were also human beings more than ten thousand years ago. These people naturally left descendants, and the descendants are very interesting on account of their culture, the most ancient on earth. Today these are the peoples called the Japanese and Chinese. They are very interesting because they are the last traces, so to say, of the oldest inhabitants of the earth.

As you have heard, there was, of course, a much older population on earth that was entirely wiped out. These were the peoples who lived in ancient Atlantis, of whom nothing remains. For even if remains did exist, we would have to dig down into the bed of the Atlantic Ocean to find them. We would have to get down to that bed—a more difficult procedure than people think—and dig there, and in all probability find nothing. For, as I have said, those people had soft bodies. Their culture, consisting of gestures, was something that one cannot dig out of the ground—because there was nothing that endured! Thus, what was there long before the Japanese and Chinese is not accessible to ordinary science; one must have some knowledge of spiritual science if one wants to make such discoveries.

However, what has remained of the Chinese and Japanese peoples is very interesting. You see, the Chinese and the older Japanese—not those of today (about whom I will speak in a moment)—the Chinese and Japanese had a culture quite different from ours. We would have a much better idea of it if we Europeans had not in recent centuries extended our domination over those regions, bringing about a complete change. In the case of Japan this change has been very thorough. Although Japan has kept its name, it has been entirely Europeanized. Its people have gradually absorbed everything from the Europeans, and what remains of their ancient culture is merely its outward form. The Chinese have preserved their identity better, but now they can no longer hold out. It is true that European dominion is not actively established there, but what the Europeans think is becoming all-prevailing, and what once existed there has disappeared. This is no cause for regret; it is in the nature of human evolution. It must, however, be mentioned.

Now if we observe the Chinese—among whom things can be seen in a less adulterated form—we find a culture distinct from all others, for the Chinese did not include in their ancient culture anything that can be called religion. The Chinese culture was devoid of religion.

You must picture to yourselves, gentlemen, what is meant by a 'culture without religion'. When you consider the cultures that have religion you find everywhere—in the old Indian culture, for instance—veneration for beings who are invisible but who seem to resemble human beings on earth. It is the peculiar feature of all later religions that they represent their invisible beings as human-like.

Anthroposophy does not do this. Anthroposophy does not represent the supersensible world anthropomorphically but as it actually is. Further, it sees in the stars the expression of the supersensible. The remarkable thing is that the Chinese had something of the same kind. The Chinese do not venerate invisible gods. They say: 'What is here on earth differs according to climate, according to the nature of the soil where one lives.' You see, China in the most ancient times was already a large country and is still today larger than Europe; it is a gigantic country, has always been gigantic, and has had a tremendously large, vigorous population. Now the idea that the population of the earth has continually increased is just superstition on the part of modern science, which always bases its calculations on data that suits itself. The truth is that even in the most ancient times there was a vast population in China, also in South America and North America. There too in those ancient times the land reached out to the Pacific Ocean. If that is taken into account the population of the earth cannot be said to have grown.

So, gentlemen, we find a culture there that is quite ancient, and today this culture can still be observed as it actually existed ten thousand, eight thousand years ago. The Chinese said: 'Above in the north the climate is different, the soil is different, from how they are farther south; everything is different there. The growth of the plants is different and human beings have to live in a different way. But the sun is all-pervading. The sun shines in the north and in the south; it goes on its way and moves from warm regions to cold regions.' And they interpreted this as meaning that on earth diversity prevails, but the sun makes everything equal. They saw in the sun a fertilizing, equalizing force. They went on to say, therefore: 'If we are to have a ruler, our ruler must be like that; individual people differ, but he must rule over them like the sun.' For this reason they gave him the name 'Son of the Sun'. His task was to rule on earth as the sun rules in the universe. The individual planets, Venus, Jupiter, and so on, act in their various ways; the sun as ruler over the planets unites and equalizes everything. Thus the Chinese pictured their ruler as a son of the sun. For they took the word 'son' essentially to imply 'belonging to something'.

Everything was then so arranged that the people said:

'The Son of the Sun is our most important man. The others are his helpers, just as the planets are the helpers of the sun'. They organized everything on earth in accordance with what appeared above in the stars. All this was done without prayer, for they did not know the meaning of prayer. It was actually all done without their having what later would constitute a cult. What might be called their kingdom was organized so as to be an image of the heavens. It could not yet be called a state. (That is a mischief which modern people perpetrate.) But they arranged their earthly affairs to be an image of what appeared to them in the stars above.

Now something came about through this circumstance that was naturally quite different from what happened later: each person became the citizen of a kingdom. He had no creed to profess; he simply felt himself to be a member of a kingdom. Originally the Chinese had no gods of any kind; when later they did have them, they were gods taken over from the Indians. Originally they had no gods, but their connection with the supersensible worlds was expressed by the essential nature of their kingdom and its institutions. Their institutions had a family quality. The Son of the Sun was at the same time father to all the other Chinese and these served him. Although it was a kingdom, it was something like a family too.

All this was only possible for people whose thinking had as yet no resemblance to that of later humanity. The thinking of the Chinese at that time was not at all like that of later human beings. How we think today would have been quite foreign to the Chinese. We think, for example, 'animal', 'man', 'vase' or 'table'. The Chinese did not think in this way, but instead: there is a lion, a tiger, a dog or a bear—not, there is an *animal*. They knew one neighbour had a table with corners; someone else had a table that was rounder. In other words they gave names to single things, but what a 'table' is never entered their head; 'table' as such — of that they had no knowledge. They could see that someone had a bigger head and longer legs, while someone else had a smaller head, with shorter legs, and so on; but 'man' in general was to them an unknown term or idea. They thought in quite a different way, in a way impossible for us today. They had need, therefore, of other concepts. Now if you think 'table', 'man', 'animal', you can extend this to legal matters, for jurisprudence consists solely of such concepts. But the Chinese were unable to think out any legal system; with them everything was organized as in a family. Within a family, when a son or daughter wants to do something, there is no thought of such a thing as a legal contract. But today, if someone here in Switzerland wants to do something, he consults liability laws, marriage laws, and so on. There one finds all that is needed, and the laws then have to be applied to individual cases.

Inasmuch as human beings still retain something of the Chinese in them — and there always remains a little — they don't really feel comfortable about laws and must always have recourse to a lawyer. They are even at sea sometimes with general concepts. As for the Chinese, they never had a legal code; they had nothing at all of what later took on the nature of a state. All they had was what each individual could judge in his individual situation.

So, to continue: the whole Chinese language was influenced by this fact. When we say 'table', we at once picture a flat surface with one, two or three legs, and so on, but it must be something that can stand up like a table. If anyone were to tell us a chair is a table, we would say: 'A table? You ass! that's not a table, that's a chair.' And if someone else came along and called the blackboard a table, we'd call him a double ass, for it's not a table at all but a blackboard. With our language we have to call each thing by its own special name.

That is not so with Chinese. I will put this to you hypothetically; it will not be a precise picture, but you will get the idea from it. Say, then, that Chinese has a certain sound for table, but this same sound signifies many other things too. Thus, let us say, such a sound might mean tree, brook, also perhaps pebble. Then it has another sound, let's say, that can mean star, and also blackboard, and—for instance— bench. (These meanings may not be correct in detail; I mean only to show the way the Chinese language is built up.) And now the Chinese person knows: there are two sounds here, say LAO and BAO, each meaning things that are quite different but also both meaning brook. So he puts them together: BAOLAO. In this way he builds up his language. He does not build it up from names given to single things, but according to the various meanings of the various sounds. A sound may mean tree but it may also mean brook. When, therefore, he combines two sounds, both of which—beside many other things—mean brook, the other man knows that he means brook. But when he utters only one sound, no one knows what he means. In writing there are the same complications. So the Chinese have an extra-ordinarily complicated language and an extraordinarily complicated script.

And indeed, gentlemen, a great deal follows from this. It follows that for them it is not so easy to learn to read and write as it is for us—nor even to speak. With us, reading and writing can really be called simple; indeed, we are unhappy when our children don't quickly learn to read and write— we think it is 'mere child's play'. With the Chinese this is not so; in China one grows quite old before one can write or in any way master the language. So you can easily imagine that the ordinary people are not at all able to do it, that only those who can go on learning up to a great age can at last become proficient. In China, therefore, noble rank is con-ferred as a matter of course on those who are cultured, and this high rank arises through the nature of the language and script. Here again it is not the same as in the West, where various degrees of nobility can be conferred and then passed on from one generation to another. In China rank can be attained only through education and scholarship.

It is interesting, gentlemen, is it not, that if we judge superficially we would surely say: 'In that case we don't want to be Chinese!' But please don't assume that I am saying we ought to become Chinese, or even particularly to admire China. That is what some people may easily say about it. Two years ago when we had a Congress in Vienna,[6] someone spoke of how some things in China were managed even today more wisely than we manage them — and immediately the newspapers reported that we wanted Chinese culture in Europe! That is not what was meant. In describing the ancient Chinese culture, praise must be given in a certain way — but only in a certain way — for what it had of spiritual content. But it was a primitive culture, of a kind that can no longer be adopted by us. So you must not think I am agitating to establish another China in Europe! I simply wish to describe this most ancient of human cultures as it actually existed.

Let us go on. What I have been saying is related to the whole manner of Chinese thinking and feeling. Indeed, the Chinese (and also the Japanese of more ancient times) occupied themselves a great deal, a very great deal, with art — with their kind of art. They painted, for instance. Now when we paint, it is quite a different affair from Chinese painting. You see, when we paint (I will make this as simple as possible), when we paint a ball, for example, if the light falls on it, then the ball is bright in one part and dark in another, for it is in shadow; the light does not fall on it. There again, on the light side, the ball is rather bright because there the light is reflected. Then we say that side is in shadow, for the light is reflected on the other side; and we also have to paint the shadow the ball throws on the ground. This is one of the characteristics of our painting: we must have light and shade on objects. When we paint a face, we paint it bright where the light falls, and on the other side we make it dark. When we paint a whole person, if we paint properly, we put shadow in the same way falling across the ground.

But beside this we must pay attention to something else in our picture. Suppose I am standing here and want to paint. I see Herr Aisenpreis sitting in front; there behind, I see Herr Meier, and the two gentlemen at the back quite small. Were I to photograph them, they would also appear quite small. When I paint, I paint in such a way that the gentlemen sitting in the front row are quite big, the next behind smaller, the next again still smaller and the one sitting right at the back has a really small head, a really small face. You see, when we paint we take perspective into account. We have to do it that way. We have to show light and shade and also perspective. This is inherent in the way we think.

Now the Chinese in their painting did not recognize light and shade, nor did they allow for perspective, because they did not see as we see. They took no notice of light and shade and no notice of perspective. This is what they would have said: 'Aisenpreis is certainly not a giant, any more than Meier is a dwarf. We can't put them together in a picture as if one were a giant and the other a dwarf, for that would be a lie, it is not the truth!' That's the way they thought about things, and they painted as they thought. When the Chinese and the Japanese learn painting in their way, they do not look at objects from the outside, they think themselves right into the objects. They paint everything from within outwards as they imagine things for themselves. This, gentlemen, constitutes the very nature of Chinese and Japanese painting.

You will realize, therefore, that learning to see came only later to mankind. Human beings in that early China thought only in pictures, they did not form general concepts like 'table' and so on, but what they saw they apprehended inwardly. This is not to be wondered at, for the Chinese descended from a culture where seeing was different. Today we see as we do because there is air between us and the object. This air was simply not there in the regions where the Chinese first became established. In the times from which the Chinese descended, people did not see in our way. In those ancient times it would have been nonsense to speak of light and shade, for there was not yet any such thing in the density the air then had. And so the Chinese still have no light and shade in their painting, and still no perspective. That came only later. From this you can see the Chinese think in quite a different way; they do not think as people do who came later.

However, this did not in the least hinder the Chinese from developing great skills and intelligence applied to the external world. When I was young – it is rather different now – we learned in school that Berthold Schwarz[7] invented gunpowder, and this was told us as if there had never been gunpowder before. So Berthold Schwarz, while he was doing alchemistic experiments, produced gunpowder out of sulphur, nitre and carbon. But the Chinese had made gunpowder thousands of years earlier!

Also we learned in school that Gutenberg[8] invented the art of printing. We did learn many things that were correct, but in this case we were led to believe that there had formerly been no knowledge of printing. Actually, the Chinese already possessed this knowledge thousands of years earlier. They also had the art of woodcarving; they could cut the most wonderful things out of wood. In such external things the Chinese had an advanced culture. This was in its turn the last remnant of a former culture still more advanced, for one recognizes that this Chinese art goes back to something even higher.

Thus it is characteristic of the Chinese to think not in concepts but in pictures, and to project themselves right into things. They have been able to make all those things which depend upon practical invention (except when it's a matter of steam-engines or something similar). So the present somewhat degenerate condition of the Chinese has actually come about from centuries of ill-treatment at the hands of the Europeans.

You see that here is a culture that is really spiritual in a certain sense—and really ancient, that goes back to ten thousand years before our time. Much later, in the millennium preceding Christianity, individuals like Laotse[9] and Confucius[10] made the first written record of the knowledge possessed by the Chinese. Those masters simply wrote down what had developed as knowledge within this old kingdom's family structure. They were not conscious of inventing rules of a moral or ethical nature; they were simply recording their experience of Chinese conduct. Previously, this had been done by word of mouth. Thus everything at that time was basically different. That is what can still be perceived today in the Chinese.

It is hardly possible to see this any longer in the old culture of the Japanese people, because they have been entirely Europeanized. They follow European culture in everything. That they did not develop this culture out of themselves can be seen from their inability to discover on their own initiative what is purely European. The following, for example, really happened. The Japanese were to have steamships and saw no reason why they should not be able to manage them perfectly well themselves. They watched how to turn the ship, for instance, how to open the screw, and so on. Their instructors, the Europeans, worked with them for a time, and finally one day the Japanese said proudly: 'Now we can manage by ourselves, and we will appoint our own captain!' So the European instructors were put ashore and off steamed the Japanese to the high seas. When they were ready to turn back, they turned the screw, and the ship turned round beautifully—but no one knew how to close the screw, and there was the ship whirling round and round on the sea, just turning and turning! The European instructors watching from the shore had to take a boat and bring the revolving ship to a standstill.

Perhaps you remember Goethe's poem 'The Magician's Apprentice' where the apprentice watches the spells of the old master-magician? And then, to save himself the trouble of fetching water, he learns a magic verse by which he will be able to make a broom into a water-carrier. One day when the old magician is out, the apprentice begins to put this magic into practice, and recites the words to start the broom working. The broom really gets down to business, and fetches water, and more water, and always more water. But the apprentice forgets how to stop it. Just imagine if you had your room flooded, and your broom went on fetching more and more water. In his desperation the apprentice chops the broom in two—then there are two water-carriers! When everything is drowned in water, the old master returns and says the right words for the broom to become a broom again.

As you know, the poem has been done in eurythmy recently, and the audience enjoyed it immensely. Well, the same kind of thing happened with the Japanese; they didn't know how to turn back the screw, and so the ship continued to go round and round. A regular ship's dance went on out there until the instructors on land could get a boat and come to the rescue.

Surely it is clear from all this that the European sort of invention is impossible for either the Chinese or the Japanese. But as to older inventions such as gunpowder, printing and so forth, they had already gone that far in much more ancient times than the Europeans. You see, the

Chinese are much more interested in their whole environment, in the world of the stars, in the universe as a whole.

Another people who point back to ancient days are the
Indians. They do not go so far back as the Chinese, but they
too have an old culture. Their culture may be said to have
arisen from the sea later than the Chinese. The people who
were the later Indian people came more from the north,
settling down in what is now India as the land became free
of water.

Now whereas the Chinese were more interested in the
world outside them, could project themselves into anything, the Indian people brooded more within themselves.
The Chinese reflected more about the world – in their own
way, but about the world; the Indians reflected chiefly
about themselves, about man himself. Hence the culture
that arose in India was more spiritualized. In the most
remote times Indian culture was still free of religion; only
later did religion enter into it. Man was their principal
object of study, but their study was of an inward kind.

This too I can best make clear by describing the way the
Indians used to draw and paint. The Chinese, looking at a
human being, painted him simply by entering into him with
their thinking – without light and shade or perspective.
That is really the way they painted him. Thus, if a Chinese
had wanted to paint Herr Burle, he would have thought his
way into him; he would not have made him dark there and
light here, as we would do today, he would not have
painted light and shadow, for they did not yet exist for the
Chinese. Nor would he have made the hands bigger by
comparison because of their being in front. But if the
Chinese had painted Herr Burle, then Herr Burle would
really have been there in the picture!

It was quite different with the Indians. When Indians
were going to paint a picture they would start by painting a
head. They too had no such thing as perspective. But they

would at once have had the idea that a head could often be different, so they would make another, then a third again different, and a fourth, a fifth would have occurred to them. In this way they would gradually have had 20 or 30 heads side-by-side! These would all have been suggested to them by the one head. Or if they were painting a plant, they imagined at once that this could be different, and then there arose a number of young plants growing out of the older one. This is how it was in the case of the Indians in those very ancient times. They had tremendous powers of imagination. The Chinese had none at all and drew only the single thing, but made their way into this in thought. The Indians had a powerful imagination.

Now you see, gentlemen, those heads are not there. Really, if you look at Herr Burle, you see only one head. If you're drawing him here on the board, you can draw only one head. You are therefore not painting what is outwardly real if you paint 20 or 30 heads; you are painting something conceived in your mind. The whole Indian culture took on that character; it was an inner culture of the mind, of the spirit. Hence when you see spiritual beings as the Indians thought of them, you see them represented with numbers of heads, numbers of arms, or in such a way that the animal nature of the body is made manifest.

You see, the Indians are quite different people from the Chinese. The Chinese lack imagination whereas the Indians have been full of it from the beginning. Hence the Indians were predisposed to turn their culture gradually into a religious one, which up to this day the Chinese have never done—there is no religion as such in China. Europeans, who are not given to making fine distinctions, speak of a Chinese religion, but the Chinese themselves do not acknowledge such a thing. They say: You people in Europe have a religion, the Indians have a religion, but we have nothing resembling a religion. This predisposition to religion was possible in the Indians only because they had a particular knowledge of something of which the Chinese were ignorant, namely, of the human body. The Chinese knew very well how to enter into something external to them. When there are vinegar, salt and pepper on our dinner table and we want to know how they taste, we first have to sample them on our tongue. For the Chinese in ancient times this was not necessary. They already tasted things that were still outside them. They could really feel their way into things and were quite familiar with what was external. Hence they had certain expressions showing that they took part in the outside world. We no longer have such expressions, or they signify at most something of a figurative nature. For the Chinese they signified reality. When I am getting to know someone and say of him 'What a sour fellow he is!' —I mean it figuratively; we do not imagine him to be really sour as vinegar is sour. But for the Chinese this meant that the person actually evoked in them a sour taste.

It was not so with the Indians; they could go much more deeply into their own bodies. If we go deeply into our own bodies, we can feel something there under certain conditions. Whenever we've had a meal and it remains in our stomach without being properly digested, we feel pain in our stomach. If our liver is out of order and cannot secrete sufficient bile, we feel pain on the right side of our body — then we are getting a liver complaint. When our lungs secrete too freely so that they are more full of mucus than they should be, then we feel there is something wrong with our lungs, that they are out of order. Today human beings are conscious of their bodies only in those organs that are sick. Those Indians of ancient times were conscious even of their healthy organs; they knew how the stomach, how the liver felt. When anyone wants to know this today, he has to take a corpse and dissect it; then he can examine the condition of the individual organs inside. No one today knows what a liver looks like unless they dissect it; it is only spiritual science that is able to describe it. The Indians could think of the interior of the human being; they would have been able to draw all his organs. With an Indian, however, if you had asked him to sense his liver and draw what he felt, he would have said: 'Liver? — well, here is one liver, here's another, and here's another,' and he would have drawn 20 or 30 livers side-by-side.

So, gentlemen, you have there a different story. If I draw a complete person and give him 20 heads, I have a fanciful picture. But if I draw a human liver with 20 or 30 others beside it, I am drawing something not wholly fantastic; it would have been possible for these 20 or 30 livers really to have existed! Every person has his distinctive form of liver, but there is no absolute necessity for that form; it could very well be different. This possibility of difference, this spiritual aspect of the matter, was far better understood by the Indians than by those who came later. The Indians said: 'When we draw a single object, it is not the whole truth; we have to conceive the matter spiritually.' So the Indians have had a lofty spiritual culture. They have never set great store by the outer world but have had a spiritual conception of everything.

Now the Indians took it for granted that learning should be acquired in accordance with this attitude; therefore, to become an educated person was a lengthy affair. For, as you can imagine, with them it was not just a matter of going deeply into oneself and then being capable of knowing everything immediately. When we are responsible for the instruction of young people, we have first to teach them to read and write, imparting to them in this way something from outside. But this was not so in the case of the ancient Indians. When they wanted to teach someone, they showed him how to withdraw into his inner depths; he was to turn his attention away from the world entirely and to focus it upon his inner being.

Now if anyone sits and looks outwards, he sees you all sitting there and his attention is directed to the outer world. This would have been the way with the Chinese; they directed their attention outwards. The Indians taught otherwise. They said: 'You must learn to gaze at the tip of your nose.' Then the student had to keep his eyes fixed so that he saw nothing but the tip of his nose, nothing else for hours at a time, without even moving his eyes.

Yes indeed, gentlemen, the European may think it terrible to train people to continually contemplate the tip of their nose! True! For the European there is something terrible in it; it would be impossible for him to do such a thing. But in ancient India that was the custom. In order to learn anything, an Indian did not have to write with his fingers; he had to look at the tip of his nose. But this sitting for hours gazing at the tip of his nose led him into his own inner being, led him to know his lungs, his liver, and so forth. For the tip of the nose is the same in the second hour as it is in the first; nothing special is to be seen there. From the tip of his nose, however, the student was able to behold more and more of what was within him; within him everything became brighter and brighter. That is why he had to carry out the exercise.

Now, as you know, when we walk about, we are accustomed to do so on our feet and this going about on our feet has an effect upon us. We experience ourselves as upright human beings when we walk on our feet. This was discouraged for students in India. While learning they had to have one leg like this and sit on it, while the other leg was in this position. Thus they sat, gazing fixedly at the tip of their nose, so that they became quite unused to standing; they had the feeling they were not upright but shrunk like an embryo in a mother's womb. You can see the Buddha portrayed in this way. It was thus that the Indians had to learn. Gradually they began to look within themselves, learned to know what is within man, came to have knowledge of the human physical body in an entirely spiritual way.

When we look within ourselves, we are conscious of our paltry thinking; we are slightly aware of our feeling but almost not at all of our willing. The Indians felt a whole world in the human being. You can imagine what different people they were from those who came later. They developed, as you know, a tremendous imagination, expressed poetically in their books of wisdom—later in the Vedas and in the Vedantic philosophy, which still fill us with awe. It figured in their legends concerning supersensible things, which still amaze us today.

And look at the contrast! Here were the Indians on the one hand, and there were the Chinese on the other, and the Chinese were a prosaic people interested in the outer world, a people who did not live from within. The Indians were a people who looked entirely inward, contemplating within them the spiritual nature of the physical body.

So—I have begun to tell you about the most ancient inhabitants of the earth. Next time I will continue, right up to the time we live in now.

Please continue to bring your questions. There may be details that you would like me to enlarge upon, and I can always, at some subsequent meeting, answer the questions you have raised. But I can't tell you when the next session will be, because now I must go to Holland. I will send you word in ten days or so.

On the relationship between foods and the human being — raw food and vegetarian diets

Rudolf Steiner: Good morning, gentlemen! Has someone thought of a question during the last weeks?

Question: I would like to ask about various foods — beans and carrots, for instance. What effect do they have on the body? You have already spoken about potatoes; perhaps we could hear something about other foodstuffs. Some vegetarians won't eat things that hang down, like beans or peas. And when one looks at a field of grain, one wonders how the various grains differ — for apparently all the peoples of the earth cultivate some grain or other.

Rudolf Steiner: So, the question is about the relation of various foods to the human body. Well, first of all we should gain a clear idea of nutrition itself. One's immediate thought of nutrition is that when we eat something, it goes through the mouth down into the stomach, then it is deposited in the body and finally we get rid of it; then we must eat again, and so on. But the process is not as simple as that. It is much more complicated. And if one wants to understand how the human being is really related to various foods, one must first be clear about the kinds of food one definitely needs.

Now the very first thing one needs, the substance one must have without fail, is protein. Let us write all this on the board, so that we have a complete overview. So, protein, as it is in a hen's egg, for instance — but not just in eggs; protein is in all foods. One definitely needs protein. The second thing one needs is fats. These too are in all foods. Plants contain fats too. The third thing has a name that will be less familiar to you, but one needs to know it: carbohydrates.

Carbohydrates are found particularly in potatoes, but they are also found in large quantity in all other plants. The important fact about carbohydrates is that when we eat them they are slowly turned into starch by the saliva in our mouth and the secretions in our stomach. Starch is something we need without fail, but we don't eat starch; we eat foods that contain carbohydrates, and the carbohydrates are turned into starch inside us. Then they are converted once again, in the further process of digestion, into sugar. And we need sugar. So you see, we get the sugar we need from the carbohydrates. But we still need something else: minerals. We get them partly by adding them to our food, for example in the form of salt, and partly they are already contained in all our food.

Now when we consider protein, we must realize how greatly it differs in animals and human beings from what it is in plants. Plants contain protein too, but they don't eat it, so where do they get it from? They get it out of the ground and out of the air, from the mineral world; they can take their protein from lifeless, mineral sources. Neither animal nor man can do that. A human being cannot use the protein that is to be got from lifeless elements — he would then only be a plant. He must get his protein as it is already available in plants or animals.

Actually, to be able to live on this earth the human being needs the plants. But now this is the amazing fact: the plants could not live on the earth either if human beings were not here! So, gentlemen, we reach the interesting fact — and we must grasp it quite clearly — that of all things the two most essential for human life are the green sap in the green leaves and blood. The green in the sap of a plant is called chlorophyll. Chlorophyll is contained in the green leaf. And the other essential thing is blood.

Now this brings us to something very remarkable. Think how you breathe — that is also a way of taking in nourishment. You take oxygen in from the air; you breathe it in. But there is carbon spread through your entire body. If you go down into the earth where there are coal deposits, you find black coal. When you sharpen a pencil, you've got graphite. Coal and graphite—they're both carbon. Your whole body is made of carbon (as well as other substances). Carbon is formed in the human body. You could say a person is just a heap of black coal! But you could also say something else. Remember the most expensive thing in the world? A diamond—and that's made of carbon; it just has a different form. And so, if you like the sound of it better, you could say you're made of glittering diamonds. The black carbon, that graphite in the pencil, and the diamonds: they are all the same substance. If someday the coal that is dug out of the earth can by some process be made transparent, you'll have diamonds. So we have diamonds hidden in our body. Or we are a coal field! But now when oxygen combines with carbon in the blood, you have carbon dioxide. And you know carbon dioxide quite well, you only have to think of Seltzer water with the bubbles in it: they are the carbon dioxide. It is a gas. So one can have this picture: a human being inhales oxygen from the air, the oxygen spreads all through his blood; in his blood he has carbon, and he exhales carbon dioxide. You breathe oxygen in, you breathe carbon dioxide out.

In the course of the earth's evolution, gentlemen, which I have recently been describing to you, everything would long ago have been poisoned by the carbon dioxide coming from human beings and animals. For this evolution has been going on a long time. As you can see, there could have been no human kingdom or animal kingdom alive on the earth for a long, long time now unless plants had had a very different character from people and animals. Plants do not take in oxygen; they take in the carbon dioxide that human beings and animals exhale. Plants are just as greedy for carbon dioxide as human beings are for oxygen.

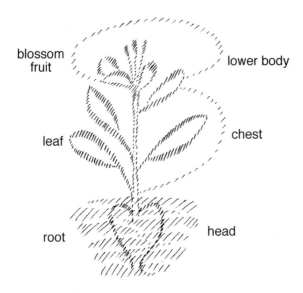

blossom fruit — lower body

leaf — chest

root — head

Now if we look at a plant [see drawing]—root, stem, leaves, blossoms—the plant absorbs carbon dioxide into every part of it. And now the carbon in the carbon dioxide is deposited in the plant, and the oxygen is breathed out by the plant. Human beings and animals get it back again. Man gives carbon dioxide out and kills everything; the plant keeps back the carbon, releases the oxygen and brings everything to life again. And the plant could do nothing with the carbon dioxide if it did not have its green sap, the chlorophyll. This green sap of the plant, gentlemen, is a magician. It retains carbon inside the plant and lets the oxygen go free. Our blood combines oxygen with carbon; the green plant-sap separates the carbon again from the carbon dioxide and sets the oxygen free. Think what an excellent arrangement nature has made, that plants and animals and human beings should complement one another in this way! They complement one another perfectly.

But that is not all. The human being not only needs the oxygen that the plant gives him, he needs the entire plant.

With the exception of poisonous plants and certain plants which contain very little of these substances, the human being needs all plants not only for his breathing but also for food. And that brings us to another remarkable connection. A plant consists of root, if it is an annual plant (we won't consider the trees at this moment) — of root, leaf and stem, blossom and fruit. Now look at the root for a moment. It is in the earth. It contains many minerals, because minerals are in the earth and the root clings to the earth with its tiny fine rootlets, so it is constantly absorbing those minerals. So the root of the plant has a special relation to the mineral realm of the earth.

And now look here, gentlemen! The part of the human being that is related to the whole earth is the head. Not the feet, but actually the head. When the human being starts to be an earthly being in the womb, he has at first almost nothing but a head. He begins with his head. His head takes the shape of the whole cosmos and the shape of the earth. And the head particularly needs minerals. For it is from the head that the forces go out that fill the human body with bones, for instance. Everything that makes a human being solid is the result of the way the head has been formed. While the head itself is still soft, as in the womb, it cannot form bones properly. But as it becomes harder and harder itself, it passes to the body the forces by which both man and animal are able to form their solid parts, particularly their bones. You can see from this that we need roots. They are related to the earth and contain minerals. We need the minerals for bone-building. Bones consist of calcium carbonate, calcium phosphate; those are minerals. So you can see that the human being needs roots in order to strengthen his head.

And so, gentlemen, if for instance a child is becoming weak in his head — inattentive, hyperactive — he will usually have a corresponding symptom: worms in his intestines.

Worms develop easily in the intestines if the head forces are too weak, because the head does not then work down strongly enough into the rest of the body. Worms find no lodging in a human body if the head forces are working down strongly into the intestines. You can see how magnificently the human body is arranged!—everything is related. And if one's child has worms, one should realize the child's head-forces are weakened. Also—whoever wants to be a teacher has to know these things—if there are persons who at a later age are weak-minded, one can be sure they had worms when they were young.

And so what must one do if one observes this in the child? The simplest remedy is to give him carrots to eat for a while—with his other food, of course; naturally, one couldn't just feed him on carrots alone. Carrots are the root of the plant. They grow down in the earth and have a large quantity of minerals. They have the forces of the earth in them, and when they are taken into the stomach, they are able to work up through the blood into the head. Only substances rich in minerals are able to reach the head. Substances rich in minerals, root substances, give strength to a human being by way of the head. That is extraordinarily important. It is through carrots that the uppermost parts of the head become strong—which is precisely what the human being needs in order to be inwardly firm and vigorous, not soft.

If you look at the carrot plant, you can't help seeing that its strength has gone particularly into the root. It is almost entirely root. The only part of the plant one is interested in is the root. The rest of it, the green part, is of no importance, it just sits there up above. So the carrot is particularly good as a food substance to maintain the human head. And if sometimes you yourselves feel empty-headed, dull, can't think properly, then it's fine if you too eat carrots for a while! Naturally, they will help children the most.

But now if we compare a potato to a carrot — well, first of all it looks quite different. Of course, the potato plant has a green part. And then it has the part we eat, what we call the tubers, deep down in the earth. Now if we would think superficially, we could say those tubers are the roots. But that is not correct; the tubers are not roots. If you look carefully down into the soil, you can see the real roots hanging on the tubers. The real roots are tiny rootlets, root hairs, that hang on the tubers. They fall away easily. When you gather up the potatoes, the hairs have already fallen away. Only in the first moment when you are lifting a potato loose from the soil, the hairs are still all over it. When we eat a potato, we are really eating a piece of swollen, enlarged stem. It only appears to be a root; in reality it is stem or metamorphosed foliage. The potato is something down there between the root and the stem. Therefore it does not have as much mineral content as the carrot; it is not as earthy. It grows in the earth, but it is not so strongly related to the earth. And it contains particularly carbohydrates; not so many minerals, but carbohydrates.

So now, gentlemen, you can say to yourselves: When I eat carrots, my body can really take it easy, for all it needs is saliva to soften the carrot. All it needs is saliva and stomach secretions, pepsin and so forth for all the important substance of the carrot to reach the head. We need minerals, and minerals are furnished by any kind of root, but in greatest amounts by such a root as the carrot.

But now, when we eat potatoes, first they go into the mouth and stomach. There the body has to exert strength to derive starch from them. Then the digestive process goes further in the intestines. In order that something can go into the blood and also reach the head, there must be more exertion still, because sugar has to be derived from the starch. Only then can it go to the head. So one has to use still greater forces. Now think of this, gentlemen: when I exert my strength upon some external thing, I become weak. This is really a secret of human physiology: that if I chop wood, if I use my external bodily strength, I become weak; but if I exert an inner strength, transforming carbohydrates into starch and starch into sugar, I become strong. Precisely through the fact that I permeate myself with sugar by eating potatoes, I become strong. When I use my strength externally, I become weak; if I use it internally, I become strong. So it is not a matter of simply filling oneself up with food, but of the food generating strength in our body.

And so one can say: food from roots — and all roots have the same effect as carrots although not to the same degree, they all work particularly on the head — food from roots gives the body what it needs for itself. Foods that lean towards the green of the plant and contain carbohydrates provide the body with strength it needs for work, for movement.

I have already spoken about the potato.* While it requires a terribly large expenditure of strength, it leaves a person weak afterwards, and does not provide him with any continuing strength. But the principle I have just given you holds good even for the potato.

Now to the same extent that the potato is a rather poor foodstuff, all the grains — wheat, rye, and so on — are good foodstuffs. The grains also contain carbohydrates, and of such a nature that the human being forms starch and sugar in the healthiest possible way. Actually, the carbohydrates of the grains can make him stronger than he can make himself by any other means. Only think for a moment how strong people are who live on farms, simply through the fact that they eat large quantities of their own homemade bread which contains the grain from their fields! They only need to have healthy bodies to start with, then if they can

---

*See next lecture for more on the potato.

digest the rather coarse bread — it is really the healthiest food for them. They must first have healthy bodies, but then they become quite especially strong through the process of making starch and sugar.

Now a question might be raised. You see, human beings have come in the course of their evolution, quite of their own accord one can say, to eat the grains differently from the way animals eat them. A horse eats his oats almost as they grow. Animals eat their kernels of grain raw, just as they come from the plant. The birds would have a hard time getting their seed if they had to depend upon someone cooking it for them first! But human beings have come of themselves to cook the grains. And now, gentlemen, what happens when we cook the grain? Well, when we cook the grain, we don't eat it cold, we eat it warm. And it's a fact, that to digest our food we need inner warmth. Unless there is warmth we can't transform our carbohydrates into starch and the starch into sugar — that requires inner heat.

So if we first apply external heat to the foodstuffs, we help the body so that it does not have to provide all the warmth itself. By being cooked first, the foods have already begun the fire process, the warmth process. That's the first result. The second is that they have been entirely changed. Think what happens to the grain when I make flour into bread. It becomes something quite different. And how has it become different? Well, first I have ground the seeds. What does that mean? I have crushed them into tiny, tiny pieces. And you see, what I do there with the seeds, grinding them, making them fine, I'd otherwise have to do later within my own body! Everything I do externally I'd otherwise have to do internally, inside my body; so by doing those things I relieve my body. And the same with the baking itself: all the things I do through cooking, I save my body from doing. I bring the foods to a condition in which my body can more easily digest them.

You have only to think of the difference if someone would eat raw potatoes instead of cooked ones. If someone were to eat his potatoes raw, his stomach would have to provide a tremendous amount of warmth to transform those raw potatoes—which are almost starch already. And the extent to which it could transform them would not be sufficient. So then the potatoes would reach the intestines and the intestines would also have to use a great amount of energy. Then the potatoes would just stay put in the intestines, for the subsequent forces would not be able to carry them farther into the body. So if one eats raw potatoes, either one just loads one's stomach with them and the intestines can't even get started on them, or one fills up the intestines; in either case there is no further digestion. But if the potatoes undergo a preparatory stage through cooking or some other means, then the stomach does not have so much to do, or the intestines either, and the potatoes enter the blood properly and continue into the head. So, you see, by cooking our foods, especially those that are counted among the carbohydrates, we are able to help our nutrition.

You are certainly acquainted with all the new kinds of foolishness in connection with nutrition—for instance, the raw food faddists, who are not going to cook anything any more, they're going to eat everything raw. How does this come about? It's because people no longer gain the knowledge they need from a materialistic science, and they shy away from a spiritual science, so they think a few things out on their own. The whole raw food fad is a fantasy. For a time someone living on raw food can whip the body along—in this situation the body has to draw on very strong forces, so you can say it needs to be whipped—but then it will collapse all the more completely.

But now, gentlemen, let us come to the fats. Plants, almost all of them, contain fats which they derive from the minerals. Now fats do not enter the human body so easily as carbohydrates and minerals. Minerals are not really changed at all. For example, when you shake salt into your soup, that salt goes almost unchanged up into your head. You get it as salt in your head. But when you eat potatoes, you don't get potatoes in your head, you get sugar. The conversion takes place as I described to you. With the fats, however, whether they're plant fats or animal fats, it's not such a simple matter. When fats are eaten, they are almost entirely eaten up by the saliva, by the gastric secretions, by the intestinal secretions, and they become something quite different that then passes into the blood. The animal and the human being must form their own fats in their intestines and in their blood, with forces which the fats they eat call forth.

You see, that is the difference between fats and sugar or minerals. The human being still takes his salt and his sugar from nature. He has to derive the sugar from the potato and the rye and so on, but there is still something of nature in it. But with the fats that man or animal have in them, there is nothing of nature left. They form them themselves. The human being would have no strength if he did not eat; his intestines and blood need fats. So we can say that man himself cannot form minerals. If he did not take in minerals, his body would never be able to build them by itself. If he did not take in carbohydrates, if he did not eat bread or something similar from which he gets carbohydrates, he would never be able to form sugar by himself. And if he could not form sugar, he would be a weakling forever. So be grateful for the sugar, gentlemen! Because you are chock-full of sweetness, you have strength. The moment you were no longer full to the brim with your own sweetness, you would have no strength, you would collapse.

And you know, that is even true of the various nationalities and peoples. There are certain peoples who consume very little sugar or foods that produce sugar. These peoples have weak physical forces. Then there are certain peoples who eat many carbohydrates that form sugar, and they are strong.

But human beings don't have such an easy time with fats. If someone has fats in him (and this is true also of the animals), that is his own accomplishment, the accomplishment of his body. Fats are entirely his own production. The human being destroys whatever fats he takes in, plant fats or animal fats, and through their destruction he develops strength. With potatoes, rye, wheat, he develops strength by converting the substances. With the fats that he eats he develops strength by destroying their substances.

If I destroy something outside of myself, I become tired and exhausted. And if I have had a big fat beefsteak and destroy that inside myself, I become weak in the same way; but my destruction of the fat beefsteak or of the plant fat gives me strength again, so that I can produce my own fat if my body is predisposed to it. So you see, the consumption of fat works very differently in the human body from the consumption of carbohydrates. The human body, gentlemen, is exceedingly complicated, and what I have been describing to you is tremendous work. Much must take place in the human body for it to be able to destroy those plant fats.

But now let us think how it is when someone eats green stuff, the stems and leaves of a plant. When he eats green stuff, he is getting fats from the plants. Why is it that sometimes a stem is so hard? Because it gives its forces to leaves that are going to be rich in carbohydrates. And if the leaves stay green—the greener they are, the more fats they have in them. So when someone eats bread, for instance, he can't absorb many fats from the bread. He takes in more, for example, from watercress—that tiny plant with very tiny leaves—more fats than when he eats bread. That's how the custom came about of putting butter on our bread, some kind of fat. It wasn't just for the taste. And why country people want bacon with their bread. There again is fat, and that also is eaten for two reasons.

When I eat bread, the bread works upon my head because the root elements of a plant work up into the stem. The stem, even though it is stem and grows above the ground in the air, still has root forces in it. The question is not whether something is above in the air, but whether it has any root forces. Now the leaf, the green leaf, does not have root forces. No green leaf ever unfolds down in the earth. In late summer and autumn, when sun forces are no longer working so strongly, the stem can mature. But the leaf needs the strongest sun forces for it to unfold; it grows towards the sun. So we can say that the green part of the plant works particularly on heart and lungs, while the root strengthens the head. The potato is also able to work into the head. When we eat greens, they chiefly give us plant fats; they strengthen our heart and lungs, the middle region, the chest.

That, I would say, is the secret of human nutrition — that if I want to work upon my head, I have roots or stems for dinner. If I want to work upon my heart or my lungs, I make myself a green salad. And in this case, because these substances are destroyed in the intestines and only their forces work on in us, cooking is not so necessary. That's why leaves can be eaten raw as salad. Whatever is to work on the head cannot be eaten raw; it must be cooked. Cooked foods work particularly on the head. Lettuce and similar things work particularly on heart and lungs, building them up, nourishing them through the fats.

But now, gentlemen, the human being must not only nurture the head and the middle body, the chest region, but he must nurture the digestive organs themselves. He needs a stomach, intestines, kidneys and a liver, and he must build up these digestive organs himself. Now the interesting fact is this: to build up his digestive organs he needs protein for food, the protein that is in plants, particularly as contained in their blossoms, and most particularly in their fruit. So we can say: the root nourishes the head particularly [see drawing p. 83]; the middle of the plant, stem and leaves, nourishes the chest particularly; and fruit nourishes the lower body.

When we look out at our grain fields we can say: Good that they are there, for that nourishes our head. When we look down at the lettuce we've planted, all those leaves that we eat without cooking because they are easily digested in the intestines — and it's their forces that we want — there we get everything that maintains our chest organs. But cast an eye up at the plums and apples, at the fruits growing on the trees — ah! those we don't have to bother to cook much, for they've been cooked by the sun itself during the whole summer! There an inner ripening has already been happening, so that they are something quite different from the roots, or from stalks and stems (which are not ripened but actually dried up by the sun). The fruits, as I said, we don't have to cook much — unless we have a weak organism, in which case the intestines cannot destroy the fruits. Then we must cook them; we must have stewed fruit and the like. If someone has intestinal illnesses, he must be careful to take his fruit in some cooked form — sauce, jam, and so forth. If one has a perfectly healthy digestive system, a perfectly healthy intestinal system, then fruits are the right thing to nourish the lower body, through the protein they contain. Protein from any of the fruits nourishes your stomach for you, nourishes all your digestive organs in your lower body.

You can see what a good instinct human beings have had for these things! Naturally, they have not known in concepts all that I've been telling you, but they have known it instinctively. They have always prepared a mixed diet of roots, greens and fruit; they have eaten all of them, and even the comparative amounts that one should have of these three different foods have been properly determined by their instinct.

But now, as you know, people not only eat plants, they eat animals too, the flesh of animals, animal fat and so on.

Certainly it is not for anthroposophy ever to assume a fanatical or a sectarian attitude. Its task is only to tell how things are. One simply cannot say that people should eat only plants, or that they should also eat animals, and so on. One can only say that some people with the forces they have from heredity are simply not strong enough to perform within their bodies all the work necessary to destroy plant fats, to destroy them so completely that then forces will develop in their bodies for producing their own fat. You see, a person who eats only plant fats—well, either he's renounced the idea of becoming an imposing, portly fellow, or else he must have an awfully good digestive system, so healthy that it is easy for him to break down the plant fats and in this way get forces to build his own fat. Most people are really unable to produce their own fat if they have only plant fats to destroy. When one eats animal fat in meat, that is not entirely broken down. Plant fats don't go out beyond the intestines, they are broken down in the intestines. But the fat contained in meat does go beyond, it passes right into the human being. And then it is fine for a person to be weaker than if he were on a diet of just plant fats.

Therefore, we must distinguish between two kinds of bodies. First there are the bodies that do not like fat, they don't enjoy eating bacon, they just don't like to eat fatty foods. Those are bodies that destroy plant fats comparatively easily and want to form their own fat. They say: 'Whatever fat I carry around, I want to make myself; I want my very own fat.' But if someone heaps his table with fatty foods, then he's not saying, 'I want to make my own fat';

he's saying, 'The world must give me my bacon.' For animal fat passes into the body, making the work of nutrition easier.

When a child sucks a sweet, he's not doing that for nourishment. There is, to be sure, something nutritious in it, but the child doesn't suck it for that; he sucks it for the sweet taste. The sweetness is the object of his consciousness. But if an adult eats beef fat, or pork fat, or the like, well, that passes into his body. It satisfies his craving just as the sweet satisfies the child's craving. But it is not quite the same, for the adult feels this craving deeper inside him. The adult needs this inner craving in order to respond to his inner being. That is why he loves meat. He eats it because his body loves it.

But it is no use being fanatic about these things. There are people who simply cannot live if they don't have meat. A person must consider carefully whether he really will be able to get on without it. If he does decide he can do without it and changes over from a meat to a vegetarian diet, he will feel stronger than he was before. That's sometimes a difficulty, obviously; some people can't bear the thought of living without meat. If, however, someone does become a vegetarian, he feels stronger — because he is no longer obliged to deposit alien fat in his body; he makes his own fat, and this makes him feel stronger.

I know this from my own experience. I could not otherwise have endured the strenuous exertion of these last 24 years! I never could have travelled entire nights, for instance, and then given a lecture the next morning. For it is a fact, that if one is a vegetarian one carries out a certain activity within one that is spared the non-vegetarian, who has it done first by an animal. That's the important difference.

But now don't get the idea that I'm making propaganda on behalf of vegetarianism! It must always be first established whether a person is able to become a vegetarian or not; it is an individual matter.

You see, this is especially important in connection with protein. One can digest protein if one is able to eat plant protein and break it down in the intestines. And then one gets the forces from it. But the moment the intestines are weak, one must get the protein externally, which means one must eat the right kind of protein, which will be animal protein. Hens that lay eggs are also animals! So protein is something that is really judged quite falsely unless it is considered from an anthroposophical point of view.

When I eat roots, their minerals go up into my head. When I eat salad greens, their forces go to my chest, lungs, and heart—not their fats, but the forces from their fats. When I eat fruit, the protein from the fruit stays in the intestines. And the protein from animal substances goes beyond the intestines into the body; animal protein spreads out. One might think, therefore, that if a person eats plenty of protein, he will be a well-nourished individual. This has led to the fact in this materialistic age that people who had studied medicine were recommending excessive amounts of protein for the average diet. They maintained that 120–150 grams of protein were necessary—which was ridiculous. Today it is known that only a quarter of that amount is necessary. And actually, if a person does eat such enormous and unnecessary amounts of protein—well, then something happens as it once did with a certain professor and his assistant.

They had a man suffering from malnutrition and they wanted to build him up with protein. Now it is generally recognized that when someone is consuming large amounts of protein—it is, of course, converted in him—his urine will show that he has had it in his diet. So now it happened in this case that the man's urine showed no sign of the protein being present in his body. It didn't occur to them that it had already passed through the intestines. The professor was in a terrible state. And the assistant was shaking in his boots as he said timidly: 'Sir — Professor — perhaps — through the intestines?' Of course!

What had happened? They had stuffed the man with protein and it was of no use to him, for it had gone from the stomach into the intestines and then out behind. It had not spread into the body at all. If one gulps down too much protein, it doesn't pass into the body at all, but into the faecal waste matter. Even so, the body does get something from it; before it passes out, it lies there in the intestines and becomes poisonous and poisons the whole body. That's what can happen from too much protein. And from this poisoning arteriosclerosis often results — so that many people get arteriosclerosis too early, simply from stuffing themselves with too much protein.

It is important, as I have tried to show you, to know these things about nutrition. For most people are thoroughly convinced that the more they eat, the better they are nourished. Of course it is not true. One is often much better nourished if one eats less, because then one does not poison oneself.

The point is really that one must know how the various substances work. One must know that minerals work particularly on the head; carbohydrates — just as they are to be found in our most common foods, bread and potatoes, for instance — work more on the lung system and throat system (lungs, throat, palate and so on). Fats work particularly on heart and blood vessels, arteries and veins, and protein particularly on the abdominal organs. The head has no special amount of protein. What protein it does have — naturally, it also has to be nourished with protein, for after all, it consists of living substances — is protein we have to form ourselves. And if one overeats, it's no use believing that in that way one is getting a healthy brain, for just the opposite is happening: one is getting a poisoned brain.

Protein:	abdominal organs
Fats:	heart and blood vessels
Carbohydrates:	lungs, throat, palate
Minerals:	head

Perhaps we should devote another session to nutrition? That would be good, because these questions are very important. So then, Saturday at nine o'clock.

Questions of nutrition—children's nutrition— hardening of the arteries—manuring

Rudolf Steiner: Today I would like to add a little more in answer to Herr Burle's question of last Thursday. You remember that I spoke of the four substances necessary to human nutrition: minerals, carbohydrates—which are to be found in potatoes, but especially in grains and legumes—then fats and protein. I pointed out how different our nutrition is with regard to protein as compared, for instance, to salt. A person takes salt into his body and it travels all the way to his head, in such a way that the salt remains salt. It is really not changed except that it is dissolved. It keeps its forces as salt all the way through to the human head. In contrast to this, protein—the protein in ordinary hens' eggs, for instance, but also the protein from plants—is at once broken down in the human body, while it is still in the stomach and intestines; it does not remain protein. The human being possesses forces by which he is able to break down this protein. He also has the forces to build something up again, to make his own protein. He would not be able to do this if he had not already broken down other protein.

Now think how it is, gentlemen, with this protein. Imagine that you have become an exceptionally clever person, so clever that you are confident you can make a watch. But you've never seen a watch except from the outside, so you cannot make a watch straight away. But if you take a chance and you take some watch to pieces, take it all apart and lay out the single pieces in such a way that you observe just how the parts relate to one another, then you can see how you are going to put them all together again.

That's what the human body does with protein. It must take in protein and take it all apart.

Protein consists of carbon, nitrogen, oxygen, hydrogen and sulphur. Those are its most important components. And now the protein is completely separated into its parts, so that when it all reaches the intestines we do not have protein in us, but carbon, nitrogen, oxygen, hydrogen and sulphur. You see how it is? — now we have the protein all laid out in its separate parts as the watch was spread out on the table. When I took that watch apart, I observed it very carefully, and now I can make watches. So you may think that I only need to eat protein once; and that after that I can make it myself. But it doesn't happen that way, gentlemen. A human being has his memory as a complete human entity. His body by itself does not have the kind of memory that can take note of something; it uses its 'memory' forces just for building itself up. So one has to continually eat new protein in order to be able to make protein.

The fact is, the human being is involved in a very, very complicated activity when he manufactures his own protein. First he divides the protein he has eaten into its separate parts and disperses the carbon from it everywhere into his body. Now you already know that we inhale oxygen from the air and that this oxygen combines with the carbon we have in us from proteins and other food elements. And we exhale carbon in carbon dioxide, retaining a part of it. So now we have that carbon and oxygen together in our body. We do not retain and use the oxygen that was in the protein; we use the oxygen we have inhaled to combine with the carbon. Thus we do not make our own protein as the materialists describe it, by eating a great many eggs which then are dispersed throughout our body, spread out through our whole body. That is not true.

Actually, we are saved by the organization of our body so that when we eat eggs we don't all turn into crazy hens! It's a fact. We don't become crazy hens because we break the protein down in our intestines, and instead of using the oxygen that was in the protein we use oxygen coming out of the air. Also, as we inhale oxygen we inhale nitrogen too; nitrogen is always in the air. Again, we don't use the nitrogen that comes to us in the hens' eggs; we use the nitrogen we breathe in from the air. And the hydrogen we've eaten in eggs, we don't use that either, not at all. Instead we use the hydrogen we take in through our nose and our ears, through all our senses; that's the hydrogen we use to make our protein. Sulphur too — we receive that continually from the air. Hydrogen and sulphur we get from the air. From the protein we eat, we keep and use only the carbon. The other substances we take from the air. So you see how it is with protein.

There is a similar situation with fat. We make our own protein, using only the carbon from protein we have ingested. And we also make our own fat. For the fats too, we use very little nitrogen from our food. So you see, we produce our own protein and fat. Only what we consume in potatoes, pulses and grains passes into our body. In fact, even these things are not fully absorbed into our body, but only to the lower parts of our head. The minerals we consume go up into the entire head; from them we then obtain what we need to build up our bones.

Therefore you see, gentlemen, we must take care to introduce healthy plant protein into our body. Healthy plant protein! That is what our body needs in large quantities. When we take in protein from eggs, our body can be rather lazy; it can easily break the protein down, because that protein is easily broken down. But plant protein, which we get from fruit — it is chiefly in that part of the plant, as I told you on Thursday — is especially valuable to us. If we want to stay healthy, it is really necessary to include fruit in our diet. Cooked or raw, but fruit we must have. If we neglect to eat fruit, we will gradually condemn our body to a very sluggish digestion.

You can see that it is also a question of giving proper nourishment to the plants themselves. And that means, we must realize that plants are living things; they are not minerals, they are something alive. A plant comes to us out of the seed we put in the ground. The plant cannot flourish unless the soil itself is to some degree alive. And how do we make the soil alive? By manuring it properly. Yes, proper manuring is what will give us really good plant protein.

We must remember that for long, long ages people have known that the right manure is what comes out of the horses' stalls, out of the cowshed and so on; the right manure is what comes off the farm itself. In recent times when everything has become materialistic, people have been saying: 'Look, we can do it much more easily by finding out what substances are in the manure and then extracting them from the mineral kingdom—mineral fertilizer!'

And you can see, gentlemen, when one uses artificial mineral fertilizer, it is as if one just put minerals into the ground; then only the root becomes strong. Then we get from the plants the substance that helps to build up our bones. But we don't get a proper protein from the plants. And the plants, our grains, have suffered from lack of protein for a long time. The lack will become greater and greater unless people return to proper manuring.

There have already been agricultural conferences in which the farmers have said: 'Yes, the quality of grain gets worse and worse!' And it is true. But naturally the farmers haven't known the reason. Every older person knows that when he was a young fellow, everything that came out of the fields was really better. It's no use thinking that one can make fertilizer simply by combining substances that are present in cow manure. One must see clearly that cow manure does not come out of a chemist's laboratory but out of a laboratory that is far more scientific — it comes from the far, far more scientific laboratory inside the cow. And for this reason cow manure is the stuff that not only makes the roots of plants strong, but also works up powerfully into the crops and produces good, proper protein in the plants which makes us healthy and vigorous.

If there is to be nothing but the mineral fertilizer that has now become so popular, or just manufactured nitrogen, obtained from the air — well, gentlemen, your children, more particularly, your grandchildren will have very pale faces. You will no longer see a difference between their faces and their white hands. Human beings have a lively, healthy colour when farmlands are properly manured.

So you see, when one speaks of nutrition one has to consider how foodstuffs are being cultivated. It is tremendously important. You can see from various circumstances that the human body itself craves what it needs. Here's just one example: people who are in jail for years at a stretch usually get food that contains very little fat, so they develop an enormous craving for fat; and when sometimes a drop of wax falls on the floor from the candle that the guard carries into a cell, the prisoner jumps down at once to lick up the fat. The human body feels the lack so strongly if it is missing some necessary substance. We don't notice this if we eat properly and regularly from day to day; then it never happens that our body is lacking some essential element. But if something is continually lacking in the diet for weeks, then the body becomes exceedingly hungry. That is also something that must be carefully observed.

I have already pointed out that many other things are connected with fertilizing. For instance, our European forefathers in the twelfth and thirteenth centuries, or still earlier, were different from ourselves in many ways. One doesn't usually pay any attention to that fact. Among other things, they had no potatoes! Potatoes were not introduced until later. The potato diet has exercised a strong influence. When grains are eaten, the heart and lungs become particularly strong. Grains strengthen heart and lungs. A person then develops a healthy chest and is in fine health. He is not so keen on thinking as on breathing, perhaps; but he can cope with a good deal when he has good breathing. And let me say right here: don't think that someone has strong lungs if he's always opening the window and crying, 'Let's get some fresh air in here!' No! A person has strong lungs if he has grown used to enduring any kind of air. The more resilient person is not the one who can't bear anything but the one who can!

Nowadays there is much talk about being hardy. Think how children are toughened up! Nowadays (in wealthy homes, of course, but then other people quickly follow suit) children's clothes only go down to the knee or are still shorter. When we were children, in contrast, we wore proper breeches and stockings and were warmly dressed — though we might, at the most, have gone barefoot occasionally. If parents knew that inadequate clothing is the best preparation for later attacks of appendicitis, they would be more thoughtful. But fashion is a tyrant! — no thought is given to the matter, and children are dressed so that their little dresses or shorts only reach to the knee, or less. Someday they will only reach to the stomach — that will be the fashion! Fashion has a strong influence.

But what is really at stake? People pay no attention to it. It is this. A human being's organism is constituted throughout so that he is truly capable of doing inner work on all the food he consumes. And in this connection it is especially important to know that a person becomes strong when he works properly on the foods he eats. Children are not made stronger by the treatment I have just mentioned. They are so 'hardened' that later in their life — just watch them! — when they have to cross an empty square with the hot sun beating down on them, they drip with perspiration and they can't manage it. Someone has not been toughened up when he is not able to stand anything; the person who can endure all possible hardships is the one who has been toughened up. So, in earlier days people were not toughened up; yet they had healthy lungs, healthy hearts, and so on.

And then came the potato diet! The potato takes little care of lung and heart. It reaches the head, but only, as I said, the lower head, not the upper head. It does go into the lower head, where one thinks and exercises critical faculties. Therefore, you can see, in earlier times there were fewer journalists. There was no printing industry yet. Think of the amount of thought expended daily in this world in our time, just to produce newspapers! All that thinking, it is much too much, it is not at all necessary — and we have to thank the potato diet for that! A person who eats potatoes is constantly stimulated to think. He can't do anything but think. That's why his lungs and his heart become weak. Tuberculosis, lung tuberculosis, did not become widespread until the potato diet was introduced. And the weakest human beings are those living in regions where almost nothing else is grown but potatoes, where people live on potatoes.

It is spiritual science that is able to examine and understand these material facts. (I have said this often.) Materialistic science knows nothing about nutrition; it has no idea what is healthy food for humanity. That is precisely the characteristic of materialism, that it thinks and thinks and thinks — and knows nothing. The truth is this, ultimately: that if one really wants to participate in life, one really needs to know something! Those are the things I wanted to say about nutrition.

And now perhaps you may still like to ask some individual questions?

Question: Dr Steiner, in your last talk you mentioned arteriosclerosis. It is generally thought that this illness comes from eating a great deal of meat and eggs and suchlike. I know someone in whom the illness began when he was 50; he had become quite stiff by the time he was 70. But now he is 85 or 86, and he is much more active than he was in his fifties and sixties. Has the arteriosclerosis receded? Is that possible? Or is there some other reason? Perhaps I should mention that this person has never smoked and has drunk very little alcohol; he has lived a really decent life. But in his earlier years he did eat rather a lot of meat. At 70 he could do very little work, but now at 85 he is continually active.

Rudolf Steiner: So — I understand you to say that this person became afflicted with arteriosclerosis when he was 50, that he became stiff and could do very little work. You did not say whether his memory deteriorated; perhaps you did not notice. His condition continued into his seventies; then he became active again, and he is still living. Does he still have any symptom of his former arteriosclerosis or is he completely mobile and active?

Questioner: Today he is completely active and more mobile than when he was 65 or 70. He is my father.

Rudolf Steiner: Well, first of all we should establish the exact nature of his former arteriosclerosis. Usually arteriosclerosis takes hold of a person in such a way that his arteries in general become sclerotic. Now if a person's arteries in general are sclerotic, he naturally becomes unable to control his body with his soul and spirit, and the body becomes rigid. Now it can also happen that someone has arteriosclerosis but not in his whole body; the disease, for instance, could have spared his brain. Then the following is the case. You see, I am somewhat acquainted with your own condition of health. I don't know your father, but perhaps we can discover something about your father's health from your own. For instance, you suffer somewhat, or have suffered (I hope it will be completely cured), from hay fever. That means that you carry in you something that the body can develop only if there is no tendency to arteriosclerosis in the head, but only outside the head. No one who is predisposed to arteriosclerosis in his entire body can possibly suffer an attack of hay fever. For hay fever is the exact opposite of arteriosclerosis. Now you suffer from hay fever. That shows that your hay fever—of course it is not pleasant to have hay fever, it's much better to have it cured; but we are talking of the tendency to have it—your hay fever is a kind of safety-valve against arteriosclerosis.

But everyone gets arteriosclerosis to a small degree. One can't grow old without having it. If one gets it in the entire body, that's different—then one can't help oneself, one becomes rigid through one's whole body. But if we get arteriosclerosis in the head and not in the rest of the body, then—well, if one is growing old properly, the etheric body is growing stronger and stronger (I've spoken of this before), and it no longer has such great need of the brain, and so the brain can now become old and stiff. The etheric body can come to control this slight sclerotic condition—which in earlier years made one old and stiff altogether; the etheric body can enable us to control it with some skill so that it is no longer so severe.

Your father, for example, does not need to have had hay fever himself; he can just have had the tendency to it. And you see, just this tendency to it has been of benefit to him. One can even say—it may seem a little far-fetched, but a person who has a tendency to hay fever can even say, 'Thank God I have this tendency! The hay fever isn't bothering me now, and it has given me the permanent predisposition to a softening of the blood vessels.' Even if the hay fever doesn't come out, it is protecting him from arteriosclerosis. And if he has a son, the son can actually

manifest the hay fever outwardly. A son can suffer externally from some disease that in the father remains latent.

Indeed, that is one of the secrets of heredity; that many
things become diseases in the descendants which in the
forefathers were aspects of health. Diseases are classified as
arteriosclerosis, tuberculosis, cirrhosis, dyspepsia, and so
forth. This can be listed and look very fine in a book; one can
describe just how these illnesses progress. But one hasn't
got very far by doing this, for the simple reason that
arteriosclerosis, for instance, is different in every single
person. No two persons have the same arteriosclerosis;
everyone becomes afflicted in a different way. That is really
so, gentlemen. And it shouldn't surprise anyone.

There were two professors[11] at Berlin University. One
was 70 years old, the other 92. The younger one was quite
well known; he had written many books. But he was a man
whose philosophy remained entirely within materialism; he
only had thoughts that were deeply entrenched in materialism. Now such thoughts also contribute to arteriosclerosis. And he got arteriosclerosis. When he reached 70,
he was obliged to retire. The colleague who was over 90 was
not a materialist; he had remained almost like a child
through most of his life, and was still teaching with tremendous liveliness. He said, 'Yes, that colleague of mine,
that young boy! I don't understand him. I don't want to
retire yet, I still feel so young.' The other one, the 'boy',
could no longer teach. Of course the 92-year-old had also
become sclerotic at his age, his arteries were completely
sclerotic, but because of his mobility of soul he could still do
something with those arteries. The other man had no such
possibility.

And now something more in answer to Herr Burle's
question about carrots. Herr Burle said, 'The human body
craves instinctively what it needs. Children often pick up a
carrot. Children, grown-ups too, are sometimes forced to

eat food that is not good for them. I think this is a mistake when someone has a loathing for some food. I have a boy who won't eat potatoes.'

Gentlemen, you need only think of this one thing: if animals did not have an instinct for what was good for them, and what was bad for them, they would all long since have perished. For animals in a pasture come upon poison-ous plants too—all of them—and if they did not know instinctively that they could not eat poisonous plants, they would certainly eat them. But they always pass them by.

But there is something more. Animals choose with care what is good for them. Have you sometimes fattened geese, crammed them with food? Do you think the geese would ever do that themselves? It is only humans who force the geese to eat so much. With pigs it is different; but how thin do you think our pigs might be if we did not encourage them to eat so much? In any case, with pigs it is a little different. They have acquired their characteristics through inheritance; their ancestors had to become accustomed to all the foods that produce fat. These things were acquired through their food in earlier times. But primeval pigs had to be forced to eat so much! No animal ever eats of its own accord what is not right for it.

But now, gentlemen, what has materialism brought about? It no longer believes in such an instinct.

I had a friend in my youth with whom I ate meals very often. We were fairly sensible about our food and would order what we were in the habit of thinking was good for us. Later, as happens in life, we lost track of each other, and after some years I came to the city where he was living, and was invited to have dinner with him. And what did I see? Scales beside his plate! I said, 'What are you doing with those scales?' I knew, of course, but I wanted to hear what he would say. He said, 'I weigh the meat they bring me, to eat the right amount—the salad too.' There he was, weighing everything he should put on his plate, because science told him to. And what had happened to him? He had weaned himself completely from a healthy instinct for what he should eat and finally no longer knew! And you remember what the textbooks used to say: 'A person needs from 120 to 150 grams of protein'; he had conscientiously weighed out this precise amount. Today the proper amount is estimated to be 50 grams, so his amount was incorrect.

Of course, gentlemen, when a person has diabetes, that is obviously a different situation. The sugar illness, diabetes, shows that a person has lost his instinct for nutrition.

There you have the gist of the matter. If a child has a tendency to worms, even the slightest tendency, he will do everything possible to prevent them. You'll be astonished sometimes to see such a child hunting for a garden where there are carrots growing, and then you'll find him there eating carrots. And if the garden is far off, that doesn't matter, the child trudges off to it anyway and finds the carrots—because a child who has a tendency to worms longs for carrots.

And so, gentlemen, the most useful thing you can possibly do is this: observe a child when he is weaned, when he no longer has milk, observe what he begins to like to eat and not like to eat. The moment a child begins to take external nourishment, one can learn from him what one should give him. The moment one begins to urge him to eat what one thinks he should eat, at that moment his instinct is spoilt. One should give him the things for which he shows an instinctive liking. Naturally, if a fondness for something threatens to go too far, one has to hold it back—but then one must carefully observe what it is that one is holding back.

For instance, perhaps in your own opinion you are giving a child every nice thing, and yet the moment that child comes to the table he cannot help jumping up on his chair and leaning over the table to sneak a lump of sugar! That's something that must be regarded in the right way. For a child who jumps up on his chair to sneak a lump of sugar obviously has something the matter with his liver. Just the simple fact that he must sneak a bit of sugar is a sign that his liver is not in order. Only those children sneak sugar who have something wrong with their livers — it is then actually cured by the sugar. The others are not interested in sugar; they ignore it. Naturally, such a performance can't be allowed to become a habit; but one must have understanding for it. And one can understand it in two ways.

You see, if a child is watching all the time and thinking, 'When will Father or Mother not be looking, so that I can take that sugar,' then later he will sneak other things. If you satisfy the child, if you give him what he needs, then he doesn't become a thief. It is of great importance from a moral point of view whether one observes such things or not. It is very important, gentlemen.

And so the question that was asked just now must be answered in this way: one should observe carefully what a child likes and what he loathes, and not force him to eat what he does not like. If it happens, for instance, as it does with very many children, that he doesn't want to eat meat, then the fact is that the child gets intestinal toxins from meat and wants to avoid them. His instinct is right. Any child who can sit at a table where everyone else is eating meat and can refuse it certainly has the tendency to develop intestinal toxins from meat. These things must be considered.

You can see that science must become more refined. Science must become much more refined! Today it is far too crude. With those scales, with everything that is carried on in the laboratories, one can't really pursue pure science.

With nutrition, which is the thing particularly interesting us at this moment, one must really acquire a proper understanding of the way it relates to the spirit. I often give two examples. Think, gentlemen, of a journalist: how he has to *think* so much – and so much of it isn't even necessary. The man must think a great deal, he must think so many logical thoughts; it is almost impossible for any human being to have so many logical thoughts. And so you find that the journalist – or any other person who writes for a profession – loves coffee, quite instinctively. He sits in the coffee shop and drinks one cup after another, and gnaws at his pen so that something will come out that he can write down. Gnawing at his pen doesn't help him, but the coffee does, so that one thought comes out of another, one thought joins on to another.

And then look at diplomats. If one thought joins on to another, if one thought comes out of another, that's bad for them! When diplomats are logical, they're boring. They must be entertaining. In society people don't like to be wearied by logical reasoning – 'in the first place – secondly – thirdly' – and if the first and second were not there, the third and fourth would, of course, not have to be thought of! A journalist can't deal with anything but finance in a finance article. But if you're a diplomat you can be talking about night clubs at the same time that you're talking about the economy of country X, then you can comment on the cream-puffs of Lady So-and-So, then you can jump to the rich soil of the colonies, after that discuss where the best horses are being bred, and so on. With a diplomat one thought must leap over into another. So anyone who is obliged to be a charming conversationalist follows his instinct and drinks lots of tea.

Tea scatters thoughts; it lets one leap from one to another. Coffee links one thought to another. If you must leap from one thought to another, then you must drink tea. And one even calls them 'diplomat teas'! Meanwhile the journalist sits in the coffee shop, drinking one cup of coffee after another. You can see what an influence a particular food or drink can have on our whole thinking process. It is so, of course, not just with those two beverages, coffee and tea — those are extreme examples. But precisely from such examples I think you can see that one must consider these things seriously. It is very important, gentlemen.

So, we'll meet again next Wednesday at nine o'clock.

On the course of humanity's cultural evolution

Rudolf Steiner: Good morning, gentlemen! A number of questions have been handed in that lead up in quite an interesting way to what we want to discuss today. Someone has asked:

'How did human civilization evolve?' I will consider this in connection with a second question:

'Why did primitive man have such a strong belief in the spirit?'

It is certainly interesting to investigate how human beings lived in earlier times. As you know, even from a superficial perspective there are two opposing opinions about this. One is that man was originally at a high level of perfection, from which he has fallen to his present imperfect state. We don't need to take exception to this, or to be concerned with the way different peoples have interpreted this perfection—some talking of paradise, some of other things. But until a short time ago the belief existed that man was originally perfect and gradually degenerated to his present state of imperfection. The other view is the one you've probably come to know as supposedly the only true one, namely, that man was originally imperfect, like some kind of higher animal, and that he gradually evolved to greater and greater perfection. You know how people point to the primitive conditions prevailing among savage peoples—so-called savage peoples—in trying to form an idea of what man could have been like when he still resembled an animal. People say: 'We Europeans and the Americans are highly civilized, while in Africa, Australia, and so on, there still live uncivilized races in their original state, or at least at a stage very near the original. From these one can study what humanity was like originally.'

But, gentlemen, this is making far too simple a picture of human evolution. First of all, it is not true that all civilized peoples imagine physical, earthly man to have been a perfect being originally. The people of India are certainly not much in agreement with opinions of our modern materialists, and yet, even so, their conception is that the physical human being who went about on the earth in primitive times looked like an animal. Indeed, when the Indians, the wise men of India, speak of man in his original state on earth, they speak of the apelike Hanuman. So you see, it is not true that even people with a spiritual world view picture primeval man similarly to the way we imagine him in paradise.

We must develop a clear knowledge that man is a being who bears within him body, soul and spirit, with each of these three parts undergoing its own particular evolution. Naturally, if people have no thought of spirit, they can't speak of the evolution of spirit. But once we acknowledge that a human being consists of body, soul *and* spirit, we can go on to ask how the body evolves, how the soul evolves, and how the spirit evolves. When we speak of the human body we will have to say: man's body has gradually been perfected from lower stages. We must also say that the evidence we have for this provides us with living proof. As I have already pointed out, we find original man in the strata of the earth, exhibiting a very animal-like body — not indeed like any present animal but nevertheless animal-like, and this must have developed gradually to its present state of perfection. There is no question, therefore, of spiritual science as pursued here at the Goetheanum coming to loggerheads with natural science, for it simply accepts the truths of natural science.

On the other hand, gentlemen, we must be able to

recognize that in the period of time of only three or four thousand years ago views prevailed from which we can learn a great deal and which we also can't help but admire. When we are guided by genuine knowledge in seriously studying and understanding the writings that appeared in India, Asia, Egypt, and even Greece, we find that the people of those times were far ahead of us. What they knew, however, was acquired in a quite different way from the way we acquire knowledge today.

Today there are many things we know very little about. For instance, from what I have told you about nutrition you will have seen how necessary it is for spiritual science to come to people's aid in the simplest nutritional matters. Natural science is unable to do so. But we have only to read what physicians of old had to say, and rightly understand it, to become aware that actually people up to the time of, for instance, Hippocrates[12] in Greece knew far more than is known by our modern materialistic physicians. We come to respect, deeply respect, the knowledge they once possessed. The only thing is, gentlemen, that knowledge was not then imparted in the same form as it is today. Today we express our knowledge in concepts. This was not so with ancient peoples; they clothed their knowledge in poetical imaginations, so that what remained of it is now just taken figuratively as poetry. It was not poetry to those people of old, but their way of expressing what they knew. Thus we find when we are able to test and thoroughly study the documents still existing that there can no longer be any question of original humanity being undeveloped spiritually. They may once have gone about in animal-like bodies, but in spirit they were infinitely wiser than we are!

But there is something else to remember. You see, when man went about in primeval times, he acquired great wisdom spiritually. His face was more or less what we would certainly call animal-like, whereas today in man's face his spirit finds expression; now his spirit is, as it were, embodied in the physical substance of his face. This, gentlemen, is a necessity if man is to be free, if he is to be a free being. These people of ancient times were very wise; but they possessed wisdom in the way the animal today possesses instinct. They lived in a dazed condition, as if in a cloud. They wrote without guiding their own hand. They spoke with the feeling that it was not they who were speaking but the spirit speaking through them. In those primeval times, therefore, there was no question of man being free.

This is something in the history of culture that constitutes a real step forward for the human race: that man acquired consciousness; that he is a free being. He no longer feels the spirit driving him as instinct drives the animal. He feels the spirit actually within him, and this distinguishes him from the people of former times.

When from this point of view we consider the 'savages' of today, it must strike us that the people of primeval times — whom the questioner called primitive man — were not like modern 'savages', but that the latter have, of course, descended from the former, from primeval human beings. You will get a better idea of this evolution if I tell you the following.

In certain regions there are people who have the idea that if they bury some small thing belonging to a sick person — for instance, bury a shirt-tail of his in the cemetery — that this can have the magical effect of healing him. I have even known such people personally. I knew one person who, at the time the Emperor Frederick[13] was ill (when he was still Crown Prince — you know all about that), wrote to the Empress (as she was later), asking for the shirt-tails belonging to her husband. He would bury them in the cemetery and the Emperor would then be cured. You can imagine how this request was received. But the man had simply done what he thought would lead to the Emperor's recovery. He himself told me about it, adding that it would have been much less foolish to let him have that shirt-tail than to send for the English Doctor Mackenzie, and so on; that had been absurd – they should have given him the shirt-tail.

Now when this kind of thing comes to the notice of a materialist he says: 'That's a superstition which has sprung up somewhere. At some time or other someone got it into his head that burying the shirt-tails of a sick man in the cemetery and saying a little prayer over it would cure him.'

Gentlemen, nothing has ever arisen in that way. No superstition arises by being thought out. It comes about in an entirely different way. There was once a time when people had great reverence for their dead and said to themselves: 'So long as a person is going about on earth he is a sinful being; beside doing good things he does many bad things.' But the dead person, they believed, lives on as soul and spirit, and death makes up for all deficiencies. Thus when they thought of the dead, they thought of what was good, and by thinking of the dead they tried to make themselves better.

Now it is characteristic of human beings to forget easily. Just think how quickly those who have left us – the dead – are forgotten today! In earlier times there were persons who would give their fellow human beings various signs to make them think of the dead and thus to improve them. Someone in a village would think that if a person was ill, the other villagers should look after him. It was certainly not the custom to collect sick-pay; that kind of thing is a modern invention. In those days the villagers all helped one another out of kindness; everyone had to think of those who were ill. The leading man in the village might say: 'People are egoists, so they have no thought of the sick unless they are encouraged to go beyond themselves and have thoughts, for instance, of the dead.' So he would tell them they should take—well, perhaps the shirt-tail of the sick person by which to remember him, and they should bury this in the earth, then they would surely remember him. By thinking of the dead they would remember to take care of someone living. This outer deed was contrived simply to help people's memory.

Later, people forgot the reason for this and it was put down to magic, superstition. This happens with very much that lives on as superstition; it has arisen from something perfectly reasonable. What is perfect never arises from what is imperfect. The assertion that something perfect can come from what is not perfect appears to anyone with insight like saying: 'Make a table, but you must make it as clumsy and unfinished as you can to begin with, so that it may in time become a perfect table.' But things don't happen that way. We never get a well-made table from one that is ill-made. The table begins by being a good one and becomes battered in the course of time. And that's the way it happens in nature too, anywhere in the world. You first have things in a perfect state, then out of them comes the imperfect. It is the same with the human being; his spirit in the beginning, though lacking freedom, was in a certain state of perfection. But his body—it is true—was imperfect. And yet precisely in this lay the body's perfection: it was soft and therefore capable of being formed by the spirit so that cultural progress could be made. Mankind, though to begin with looked more animal-like, was highly civilized.

Now perhaps you will ask: But were those original animal-like people the descendants of apes or of other animals? That is a natural question. You look at the apes as they are today and think we are descended from those apes. But when human beings had their animal form, there were no such animals as our present apes! Human beings have therefore not descended from the apes. On the contrary! The apes are beings who have regressed.

On going back further in the evolution of the earth, we find human beings formed in the way I described here recently, developing out of a soft element—not from our present animals. Human beings could never evolve out of the apes of today. On the other hand it could easily be possible that if conditions prevailing on earth today continue, conditions in which everything is based on violence and power, and wisdom counts for nothing—well, it could indeed happen that those who want to found everything on power would gradually take on animal-like bodies again, and that two races would then appear. One race would be those who stand for peace, for the spirit, and for wisdom, while the other would be those who revert to an animal form. It might indeed be said that those who care nothing today for the progress of mankind, for spiritual realities, may be running the risk of degenerating into an ape-type species.

You see, we experience all manner of strange things nowadays. Of course, what newspapers report is largely untrue, but sometimes it shows the trend of people's thinking in a remarkable way. During our recent trip to Holland we bought an illustrated paper, and on the last page there was a curious picture: a child, a small child, really a baby—and as its nurse, taking care of it, bringing it up, an ape, an orang-utan. There it was, holding the baby quite properly, and it was going to be engaged, the paper said—somewhere in America, of course—as a nursemaid.

Now it is possible that this may not yet be actual fact, but it shows what some people imagine: they would like to use apes today as nursemaids. And if apes become nursemaids, gentlemen, what an outlook for mankind! Once it is discovered that apes can be employed to look after children (it is, of course, possible to train them to do many things, the child will have to suffer for it, but the ape could be trained to do this; in certain circumstances it could be trained to look after the physical needs of children), well, then people will carry the idea further and the social question will arrive at a new level. You will see far-reaching proposals for breeding apes and putting them to work in factories. Apes will be found to be cheaper than human beings, hence this will be looked upon as the solution of the social question. If people really succeed in having apes look after their children — well, we'll be deluged by pamphlets on how to solve the social question by breeding apes!

It is indeed conceivable that this might happen. Only think: other animals beside apes can be trained to do many things. Dogs, for instance, can be taught. But the question is whether this will be for the advance or the decline of civilization. Civilization will most definitely decline. It will deteriorate. Children brought up by ape-nurses will quite certainly become apelike. Then indeed we shall have perfection changing into imperfection. We must realize clearly that it will indeed be possible for certain human beings to have an apelike nature in the future, but that the human race in the past was never such that mankind evolved from the ape. For when man still had an animal form — quite different indeed from that of the ape — the present apes were not yet in existence. The apes themselves are degenerate beings; they have declined from a higher stage.

When we consider those ancient primitive peoples who may be said to have been rich in spirit but animal-like in body, we find they were still undeveloped in reason, in intelligence — the faculty of which we are so proud. Those people of ancient times were not capable of thinking. Hence, when anyone today who prides himself particularly on his thinking comes across ancient documents, he searches for the thought underpinning them — and looks in vain. He says, therefore: 'This is all very beautiful, but it's simply poetry.' But, gentlemen, we can't judge everything by our own standards alone, for then we go astray. That ancient humanity had, above all, great powers of imagination, an imagination that worked like an instinct. When we use our imagination nowadays we often pull ourselves up short, thinking that imagination has no part in what is real. This is quite right for us today, but the people of primeval times, primitive people, would never have been able to survive without imagination.

Now it will seem strange to you how this lively imagination possessed by primitive people could have been applied to anything real. But here too our conceptions are wrong. In your history books at school you will have read about the tremendous importance for human evolution ascribed to the invention of paper. The paper we write on — made of rags — has been in existence for only a few centuries. Before that, people had to write on parchment, which has a different origin. Only at the end of the Middle Ages did someone discover the possibility of making paper from the fibres of plants, fibres worn threadbare after having first been used for clothes. Human beings were late in acquiring the intellect that was needed to make this paper.

But the same thing (except that it is not as white as we like it for our black ink) was discovered long ago. The same stuff as is used for our present paper was discovered not just two or three thousand years ago but many, many thousands of years before our day. By whom, then? Not by human beings at all, but by wasps! Just look at any wasps' nest you find hanging in a tree. Look at the material it consists of — paper! Not white paper, not the kind you write on, for the wasps have not developed the habit of writing, otherwise they would have made white paper, but such paper as you might use for a parcel. We do have a drab-coloured paper for parcels that is just what the wasps use for making their nests. The wasps found out how to make paper thousands and thousands of years ago, long before human beings arrived at it through their intellect.

The difference is that instinct works in animals while in the human beings of primeval times it was imagination; they would have been incapable of making anything if imagination had not enabled them to do so, for they lacked intelligence. We must therefore conclude that in outward appearance these primeval people were more like animals than are the people of today, but to a certain extent they were possessed by the spirit, the spirit worked in them. It was not they who possessed the spirit through their own powers, they were possessed by it and their souls had great power of imagination. With imagination they made their tools; imagination helped them in all they did, and enabled them to make everything they needed.

We, gentlemen, are terribly proud of all our inventions, but we should consider whether we really have cause to be so; for much of what constitutes the greatness of our culture has actually developed from quite simple ideas. For instance, when you read about the Trojan War, do you realize when it took place? About 1200 years before the founding of Christianity, not in Greece, but far away in Asia. Nowadays we would hear the outcome of such a war the next day in Greece by telegram; but that, gentlemen, didn't happen in those days! Today if we receive a telegram, the Post Office dispatches it to us. Naturally this didn't happen at that time in Greece, for the Greeks had no telegraph. So what could they do? Well, you see, the war was over here in one place; then there was the sea and an island, a mountain and again sea; over there another island, a mountain and then sea; and so on till you came to Greece—here Asia, then sea, and there Greece. It was agreed that when the war ended, three fires would be kindled on each range of mountains. Whoever was posted on the nearest mountain was to give the first signal by running up and lighting three fires. The watch on the next mountain, upon seeing the three fires, lit three fires in his turn. The next watchman again lit three fires, and in this way the message arrived in Greece in quite a short time. This was their method of sending a telegram. It was done like that. It's a simple way of telegraphing. It worked fast — and before the days of the telegraph people had to make do with this.

And how is it today? When you telephone — not telegraph but telephone — I will show you in the simplest possible way what happens. We have a kind of magnet which, it is true, is produced by electricity; and we have something called an armature. When the circuit is closed, this is pulled shut; when the circuit is open, the armature is released, and thus it oscillates back and forth. It is connected by a wire with a plate, which vibrates with it and transmits what is generated by the armature — in just the same way as in those olden times the three fires conveyed messages to people. This is rather more complicated, and, of course, electricity has been used in applying it, but it is still the same idea.

When we hear such things we must surely respect what the human beings of those ancient times developed and devised through their imaginative faculty. And when we read the ancient documents with this feeling we must surely say that those people accomplished great things on a purely spiritual level and all through imagination. To come to a thorough realization of this you need only consider what people believe today. They believe they know something about the old Germanic gods — Wotan, Loki, for instance. You find pictures of them in human form in books: Wotan with a flowing beard; Loki looking like a devil, with red hair, and so on. It is thought that the people of old, the ancient Germans, had the same ideas about Wotan and Loki. But that is not true. Instead they had the following conception. When the wind blows, they believed, there is something spiritual in it — which is indeed true — and that is Wotan blowing in the wind. They never imagined that when they went into the woods they would meet Wotan there in the guise of an ordinary man. To describe a meeting with Wotan they would have spoken of the wind blowing through the woods. This can still be felt in the very word *Wotan* by anyone who is sensitive to these things. And Loki — they had no image of Loki sitting staring in a corner; no, Loki lived in fire!

Indeed, in various ways people were always talking about Wotan and Loki. Someone would say, for instance: 'When you go over the mountain, you may meet Wotan. He will make you either strong or weak, whichever you deserve.' That is how people felt, how they understood these things. Today one says that's just superstition. But in those times they didn't understand it to be so. They knew that if you climbed up to a certain inaccessible place, you wouldn't meet a man in a body like any ordinary man but the very shape of the mountain would rise to a special whirlwind there and a special kind of air, which you might experience, is wafted up to that place from an abyss. If you withstand this and keep to your path, they believed, you may become well or you may become ill. In what way you become well or ill, the people were ready to tell; they were in harmony with nature and would speak not in an intellectual way but out of their imagination. Your modern doctor would try to express himself in more intellectual terms, such as: 'If you have a tendency to tuberculosis, go up to a certain height on the mountain and sit there every day. Continue to do this for some time, for it will be most beneficial.' That is the intellectual way of talking. But if you speak imaginatively you say: 'Wotan is always to be found in that high place; if you visit him at a certain time every day for a couple of weeks, he will help you.'

This is the way people grasped life through their imagination. They worked in this way, too. Surely at some time or other you have all been far into the the country where threshing is not done by machine but is still being done by hand. You can hear the people threshing in perfect rhythm. They know that when they have to thresh for days at a time, if they go at their work without any order, just each one on his own, they will very soon be overcome by exhaustion. Threshing can't be done that way. If, however, they work rhythmically, all keeping time together, they keep their strength up—because their rhythm is then in harmony with the rhythm of their breathing and circulation. It even makes a difference whether they strike their flail on the out-breath or the in-breath or whether they do it as they are changing over from one to the other. Now why is this? You can see that it has nothing to do with intellect, for today this old way of threshing is almost unheard of. Everything of that kind is being superseded. But in the past, all work was done rhythmically and out of imagination. The beginnings of human culture developed out of rhythm.

Now I don't suppose you really think that if you take a chunk of wood and some bits of string and fool about with them in some amateurish fashion you'll suddenly have a violin. A violin comes about when mind, when spirit, is exerted, when the wood is carefully shaped in a particular way, when the string is put through a special process, and so forth. We have to say therefore that these primeval people, who were not yet thinking for themselves, could attribute the way they made instruments or machines only to the spirit that possessed them, that worked in them. So these people, working not out of the intellect, but out of their imagination, naturally tended to speak of the spirit everywhere, indwelling everything.

When today someone constructs a machine through his intellect, he does not say that the spirit helped him—and rightly so. But when a person of those ancient times who knew nothing about thinking, who had no capacity for thinking, when that person constructed something, he felt immediately: the spirit is helping me.

It happened therefore that when the Europeans, those 'superior' beings, first arrived in America and also later, in the nineteenth century, when they came to the regions where native Indians descended from ancient times were still living, these Indians spoke of the 'Great Spirit' ruling everywhere, ruling in everything. It was this 'Great Spirit' that was venerated particularly by the human beings alive in Atlantean times when there was still land between Europe and America; the Indians retained this veneration, and knew nothing as yet of intellect. They then came gradually to know the 'superior' people—before being exterminated by them. They came to know the Europeans' printed paper on which there were little signs which they took to be small devils. They abhorred the paper and the little signs, for these were intellectual in origin, and a man whose activities arise out of imagination abominates what comes from the logical intellect.

Now the European with his materialistic civilization knows how to construct a locomotive. The intellectual method by which he constructs his engine could never have been the way the ancient Greeks would have set about it, for the Greeks still lacked intellect. Intellect first came to man in the fifteenth and sixteenth centuries. The Greeks would have carried out their construction with the help of their imagination. Since the Greeks ascribed all natural forms to good spirits and all that is not nature, all that is artificially produced, to bad spirits, they would have said: 'An evil spirit lives in the locomotive.' They would certainly have contrived their construction from imagination; nothing else would ever have occurred to them than that they were being aided by the spirit.

Therefore, gentlemen, you see that we have actually to ascribe a lofty spirit to the original, primitive human being; for imagination is of a far more spiritual nature in the human soul than the mere intellect that is prized so highly today.

Former conditions, however, can never return. We have to go forward — but not with the idea that what exists today in the animal as pure instinct could ever have developed into spirit. We should not, therefore, picture primitive people as having merely possessed instinct. They knew that it was the spirit working in them. That is why they had, as we say nowadays, such a strong belief in the spirit.

Perhaps this contributes a little to our understanding of how human culture has evolved. Also, we must concede that the people are right who argue that human beings have arisen from animal forms, for so indeed they have — but not from such forms as the present animals, for these forms only came into being later, when humanity was already in existence. The early animal-like forms of man which gradually developed in the course of human evolution into his present form, together with the faculties which he already had at that time, came about because man's spiritual entity was originally more perfect than it is today — not in terms of intellect but of imagination. We should always remember that this original perfection was due to the fact that man was not free; man was, as it were, possessed by the spirit. Only intellect enables man to become free. By means of his intellect man can become free.

You see, anyone who works with his intellect can say: 'Now at a certain hour I'm going to think out such and such a thing.' This can't be done by a poet, for even today a poet still works out of his imagination. Goethe was a great poet. Sometimes when someone asked him to write a poem or when he himself felt inclined to do so, he sat himself down to write one at a certain time — and, well, the result was pitiful! That people are not aware of this today comes simply from their inability to distinguish good poetry from bad. Among Goethe's poems there are many bad ones. Imaginative work can be done only when the mood for it is there, and when the mood has seized a poet he must write the poem down at once. And that's how it was in the case of primeval humans. They were never able to do things out of free will. Free will developed gradually—but not wisdom. Wisdom was originally greater than free will and it must now regain its greatness. That means we must return to the spirit by way of the intellect.

And that, you see, is the task of anthroposophy. It has no wish to do what would please many people, that is, to bring primitive conditions back to humanity—ancient Indian wisdom, for example. It is nonsense when people harp on about that. Anthroposophy, on the other hand, sets value on a return to the spirit, but a return to the spirit precisely in full possession of the intellect, with the intellect fully alive. It is important, gentlemen, and must be borne strictly in mind, that we have nothing at all against the intellect; rather, the point is that we have to go forward with it. Originally human beings had spirit without intellect; then the spirit gradually fell away and intellect increased. Now, by means of the intellect, we have to regain the spirit. Culture is obliged to take this course.

If it does not do so—well, gentlemen, people are always saying that the World War was unlike anything ever experienced before, and it is indeed a fact that human beings have never before so viciously torn one another to pieces. But if they refuse to embark on a return to the spirit that at the same time retains their intellect, then still greater wars will come upon us, wars that will become more and more savage. People will really destroy one another as the two rats did that, shut up together in a cage, gnawed at each other till there was nothing left of them but two tails.

That is putting it rather brutally, but in fact mankind is on the way to total annihilation. It is very important to know this.

The sense of smell

Rudolf Steiner: Good morning, gentlemen! Perhaps someone has a question? We will not be able to meet again for a
little while.

Herr Erbsmehl: I have a rather complicated question. I don't
quite know how to put it. One knows that plants have
different scents. This is also true of the various human races.
You have already spoken to us, Dr Steiner, about the evolution of humanity. A factor in this evolution must have
been that each kind of being acquired what would benefit it.
Different smells can be associated with the various races, so
there must be some spiritual connection. Just as the plants
have their scent from the earth, so the different races of
human beings must have acquired their smell. How does
this relate to human evolution?

Rudolf Steiner: I will try to put the question in a way that
will lead to what you may have in mind. You have been
thinking, have you not, of different kingdoms of nature:
plants, animals, human beings. Also, we must not forget,
minerals have different odours. Now smell is only one
sense-perception and there are many other kinds. So perhaps we could ask how the different smells belonging to the
different beings of nature are related to the origin and
evolution of these beings.

Well, let us first consider what causes smell. What is
smell? You must realize first of all that people have varying
reactions to a smell coming from an object or from other
products of nature. For instance, in a place where people are
drinking wine, someone who is a wine-drinker himself
hardly notices the smell, while someone who never touches

wine finds it extremely unpleasant either to be in a room where others are drinking wine or in a place where wine is stored. It is the same with other things. For instance, there are people, usually women, who can't stay in a room where there is a dog even for a short time without getting a headache. Different beings, therefore, are sensitive to smells in different ways. This makes it difficult to get at the truth.

But what has been said applies not only to smell; it applies equally to other sense-perceptions. Imagine for a moment that, standing where you are, you put your hand into water of, say 79° or 80° Fahrenheit. The water will not seem particularly cold. But if you have previously had your hand for some time in water of 86° and then you plunge it into water of 80°, the water will seem colder than it did before. We can take this further. Think of a red surface. If the background is white, the red will seem very vivid to you. But if you paint the background blue, the red surface will lose some of its vividness. Everything, therefore, depends very largely upon how the human being himself relates to things. This has led to the opinion that the human being does not perceive objects in themselves but only the effect they have upon him. We have spoken of this before. But we must get to the truth behind such things.

There is no question that a violet is easily distinguishable from the asafoetida by its smell. The violet has a scent that is always pleasant; the asafoetida has a smell that is offensive, that we want to avoid. It is also correct that different races have different smells. Someone with, shall I say, a sensitive nose will certainly be able to distinguish a Japanese from a European by their smell.

Now we must be clear as to what it is that causes smell. The fact of the matter is that any object with a smell or scent emits something that comes towards our own body in a gaseous or airy form. When nothing of this kind comes towards us, we cannot smell the object. And these gaseous substances must come into contact with our organ of smell, our nose. We can't smell a liquid as liquid, we can only taste it. We can smell a liquid only when it emits air, that is to say, gaseous substance. We don't smell our foodstuffs because they are fluid but because they emit air which then passes into us through our nose.

There are people who can't smell at all. The whole world is devoid of smell as far as they are concerned. Only recently I met a man whose incapacity to smell is a severe handicap to him because his work requires that he should be able to distinguish things by their scent. His defect is a grave disadvantage. The cause is, of course, imperfectly developed olfactory nerves.

And now let us ask: how is it that bodies or objects emit gas which may have a particular smell? Objects or bodies can be classified. There are solid bodies (they were called earthy bodies in earlier times); there are fluid bodies (they were called watery bodies in earlier times). People used to call water what we no longer classify as water. In earlier times everything fluid was called water, even quicksilver. Then there are gaseous or aeriform bodies. If we think of these three kinds of bodies — solid, fluid and gaseous — one fact is particularly striking. Water is certainly fluid, but when it freezes to ice it becomes a solid body. A metal — lead, for instance — is solid, but when you heat the lead sufficiently it becomes fluid, like water. So these different substances — solid, fluid, gaseous substances — can be transferred into the other conditions. Even air can be solidified today, or in any case liquefied, and there is every expectation of being able to carry this further. Any object or body can be either solid, fluid or gaseous.

Any object that has a smell contains gas imprisoned, as it were, within it. We don't smell a solid body as such or a fluid body as such; we always smell a gas. But now, a violet is certainly not a gaseous body and yet we can smell it. Of what is a violet composed? It is obviously solid, yet it has scent. We must picture to ourselves that it contains solid constituents and between them something that vapourizes as gas. The violet contains gas that can vapourize. In order that this may be possible, the violet must be attracted to certain forces. When you pick a violet, you really only pick the solid part of it and you look at this solid part. But actually the violet does not only consist of the solid part that you pick. What the violet is, is enshrined in this solid part. One can say that the real violet, that which gives forth the fragrance, is actually a gas. It is there within the petals and the other parts of the flower — just as you stand in your shoes or boots. You are not your boots. And what has fragrance in the violet is not its solid part but its gaseous part.

When people look out into the universe they think that space is empty and that the stars are in this empty space. In times gone by, peasants believed that there was emptiness all around them as they moved about. Today everyone knows that there is air around us, not emptiness. So, too, we can know that in the universe there is no emptiness anywhere; either matter is there or spirit is there. It can be demonstrated that there is no emptiness anywhere in the universe. This is interesting to think about. I will prove it to you by an example.

For the moment let us disregard what Copernicus taught, namely, that the earth revolves around the sun; let us take things as they appear.[14] We have the earth with the sun moving around it, rising in the east and setting in the west. The sun is always at a different point. But there is something remarkable here. In certain regions — but everywhere, really; one only has to observe carefully — at sunrise and at sunset, other times too, there is not only twilight but something else that is always a thing of wonder. Around the sun there is a kind of radiating light. Whenever we look at the sun, but especially towards morning and evening, this radiating light is apparent as well as the twilight. Light radiates around the sun. It has a name: the zodiacal light. People rack their brains about this zodiacal light — especially those who think in a materialistic way. They say to themselves: 'The sun shines in empty space and when it shines, it illumines other celestial bodies, but where does this zodiacal light around the sun come from?' Countless theories have been put forward as to its origin. Whether one assumes that the sun moves around through empty space, or — as Copernicus taught — merely stands still, this does not account in any way for the presence of that light. So where does the light come from?

This is a very simple matter to explain. You will certainly have walked through the town on a very clear evening and seen the street lamps. On a clear evening the lights have definite outlines. But on a misty, foggy evening there is always a haze of light around them. Why is this? The haze is caused by mist. At certain times the sun moves across the sky in a haze because heavenly space is not empty but filled with fine mist. The radiance that is present in this fine mist is the zodiacal light. All kinds of explanations have been given: for example, that comets are always flashing through space out there. And so, of course, they are. But the reason why this zodiacal light that accompanies the sun is sometimes strong, sometimes faint, sometimes not visible at all is that the mist in the universe is sometimes dense and sometimes thin. Thus we can say that the whole of cosmic space is filled with something.

But as I have already told you, it is not correct to think that there is substance or matter everywhere. I have told you that materialistic physicists would be immensely astonished if they went up into space expecting to find the sun as they describe it in their science. Their descriptions are nonsense. If by some convenient means of transport the physicists could reach the sun, they would be amazed to find no gas whatsoever. They would find hollow space, a real vacuum. This vacuum radiates light. And what they would find is spirit. We cannot say there is only matter everywhere; we must say there is also spirit everywhere, real spirit. So you see, everything on the earth is affected from outer space, not only by matter but also by spirit.

And now, gentlemen, let us consider how the spiritual is connected with the physical in man.

There is a creature familiar to us all that has a better sense of smell than you or I, namely, the dog. Dogs have a much more delicate sense of smell than human beings. And you know to what use this is put nowadays. Think of the police dogs that use their sense of smell to find people who have run away after committing some crime. The dog picks up a scent at the spot where the crime was committed and follows it until it leads to the criminal. The dog has very delicate olfactory nerves. It is extremely interesting to study this fine sense perception and to see how these olfactory nerves are connected with the rest of the dog's organism. Behind its nose, in its brain, the dog has a very interesting organ of smell. Its nose is only one part. The larger part of a dog's organ of smell is situated behind the nose, in the brain.

Now let us compare the dog's organ of smell with that of the human being. The dog has a brain that is clearly made for smelling, a brain that becomes an organ of smell. In the human being the greater part of this 'smell-brain' has been transformed into an 'intelligence-brain'. We understand things; the dog doesn't understand things, he smells them. We understand them because at the place where the dog has his organ of smell that organ is transformed in us. Our organ of intelligence is a transformed organ of smell. In us there is only a tiny remnant left of this 'smell-brain'. That is why our sense of smell is inferior to the dog's. And so you can imagine that when a dog runs over the fields he finds everything terribly interesting; so many smells come to him that if he were able to describe it he would say the world is all smell. If among dogs there were a thinker like Schopenhauer,[15] he would write interesting books! Schopenhauer wrote a book called 'The World as Will and Idea' — but he was a man and his organ of smell had become an organ of thinking. The dog could write a book called 'The World as Will and Smell'. In the dog's book there would be a great deal beyond the discernment of a human being, because while a human being forms an idea, a mental image of things, a dog smells them. And it is my private opinion that the dog's book — if the dog were a Schopenhauer — would actually be more interesting than the book that Schopenhauer himself wrote!

So you see how it is. We live in a world that can be smelled, and other creatures — the dog, for instance — are much more acutely aware of this than we are.

Now since the universe is filled with the gaseous substance we perceive in the zodiacal light, this universe would be found to emit all kinds of different smells if organs of smell existed which were even more delicate than that of the dog. Imagine some creature sniffing towards the sun, not seeing the beauty of the sun but becoming aware through its sniffing of how the sun smells. Such a creature would not say as the poets do, 'The lovers went a-roaming in the enchanting moonlit night,' but he would say, 'The lovers went a-roaming in the enchanting moon-scented night, in a world of sweet fragrance,' or perhaps, since it's to do with the moon, the scents would not be so very pleasantly fragrant! Again, such a creature might sniff towards the evening star, and its smell would be different from that of the sun. Then it might sniff towards Mercury, towards Venus, towards Saturn.

It would have no picture of these stars like that transmitted through the eyes, but it would get the sun smell, the moon smell, the Saturn smell, the Mars smell, the Venus smell. If there were such creatures, they would be guided by what the spirit inscribed in the smell of the cosmic gas, by what the spirit of Venus, Mercury, sun, moon inscribes into world existence.

But now, gentlemen, think of fish. Fish don't smell things. But they take on colours according to how the sun shines upon them. They reflect in their own colouring what comes to them from the sun. So you see, a being with a very delicate sense of smell would actually adjust its being to the way it smells the universe.

Such beings do exist. There are beings that can actually smell the universe, and these are the plants. The plants smell the universe and adapt themselves accordingly. What does the violet do? The violet is really all nose, a very, very delicate nose. The violet is beautifully aware of what streams from Mercury and forms its scent-body accordingly, while the asafoetida has a delicate perception of what streams from Saturn and forms its gas-body accordingly, thereby acquiring an offensive odour. And so it is that every being in the plant world perceives the smells that come from the planetary world.

But now what about plants that have no fragrance? Why have they no scent? As a matter of fact, to sensitive noses all plants do have a certain scent—at the least, they have what can be called a refreshing aroma—and this has a very strong effect upon them. This refreshing fragrance comes from the sun. A large number of plants are only receptive to this sun smell. But various plants, like the violet or the asafoetida, are receptive to planetary influences; these are the sweet-smelling or the bad-smelling plants.

And so, when we smell a violet, we can say that this violet is really all nose—but a delicate nose, inhaling the cosmic scent of Mercury. It holds the scent, as I have indicated, between its solid parts and exhales it; then the scent is dense enough for us to be able to smell it. So when Mercury comes towards us through the violet, we smell Mercury. If with our coarse noses we were to sniff towards Saturn, we would smell nothing. But when the asafoetida, which has a keen nose for Saturn, sniffs towards that planet, it smells what comes from it, adapts its gas content accordingly, and has a most foul odour. Suppose you are walking through an avenue of horse-chestnuts—you know the scent of horse-chestnut, or of linden blossoms? They both have such perfume because their flowers are sensitive noses for everything that streams into the universe from Venus. And so in very truth the fragrances of heaven come to us through the plants.

Now let us turn to something else Herr Erbsmehl mentioned in his question, namely, the human races. Originally, different races lived in different regions of the earth. One race developed in one region, another race in another. Why was this? It is quite correct to say that one planet has a particularly strong influence upon one part of the earth, another planet upon another part. In Asia, for instance, the land is strongly affected by what streams to the earth from Venus—Venus, the evening star. What streams from Saturn works with particular strength upon American soil. And Mars works particularly strongly upon Africa. So we find that each of the planets works particularly strongly upon some specific part of the earth. They radiate their light from the various places where they stand in the heavens. The light of Venus, for instance, works quite differently upon the earth than does the light of Mercury. This is connected with the different formations of mountains, of rocks. Thus the different races inhabiting different regions of the earth are dependent upon the fact that one part of the earth is particularly receptive to the influences of Venus, another part to the influences of Saturn, and so on. And the plant-nature man contains is determined in accordance with this.

The human being has the whole of nature within himself: mineral, plant, animal and man. The plant-nature in the human being adjusts itself to the scents of the planets just as do the plants themselves. Certain minerals that still retain much of the plant-nature also have an odour. So whether something does or does not have an odour depends upon whether it perceives the scents of the universe.

It is very important that you should understand these things, for people talk today about plants having perception, having a soul like human beings. That, of course, is nonsense. I spoke about it once. There are plants—like the one called Venus' fly-trap[16]—that are supposed to have feeling. When an insect comes close enough, the 'trap' closes and the insect is caught. It would be just as logical to say that a mousetrap has a soul, for the reason that when a mouse comes close enough, the trap shuts and the mouse is caught! External aspects like this should be ignored if one wants to acquire real knowledge. If knowledge is our aim, we must get to the root of things. Thus, if we know that with their fragrance plants are breathing out what they inhale from the universe, then we can say that plants are the delicate organs of smell that belong to the earth. And the human nose, gentlemen—that's really a coarse plant. It grows out of man like a kind of blossom, but it has become coarse. It is a coarse flower that grows out of the human being. It no longer has such delicate perception as the plants. These are pictures, of course, but they are true. And it's the way things are.

So we can say: wherever we go in the world of plants, we find the earth covered with noses—the plants. But it never occurs to us that our own strange noses really derive from the plants. As a matter of fact, many blossoms look like a human nose. There are indeed such plants—the snapdragons, also the Labiates—they look just like a nose. You find them growing everywhere.

In this way we attain true knowledge of the world. And we discover how mankind is indeed related to all the rest of the universe. It might well be said, man is a poor creature; he has a nose for smelling, but he can't smell much because his nose has become too coarse, whereas the blossoms of plants can smell the whole universe. The leaves of plants can be compared to the human tongue; they can taste the world. The roots of plants can be compared to the organ in man that looks at things, his eyes, but in man it's a weak organ. Poor human being! He has everything that the beings of outer nature have, but in him it has all grown feeble.

But now, gentlemen, we sometimes come across strange things. If we were able to smell as keenly as the plants smell and were able to taste as delicately as their leaves taste — well, we wouldn't know where we were, for scents and tastes would come at us from every direction! We wouldn't have to eat anything in order to experience taste because taste would stream towards us from all sides. But this does not happen to us. Man no longer has such perceptions. Instead, he has his intelligence. Think of an animal that has a 'smell-brain' strongly developed behind its nose. In the human being this kind of brain is stunted and his nose has become coarse; it is just a shrunken remnant. But instead, he has his reasoning brain. It is the same with his organ of taste. Most animals have a brain highly developed for tasting; they can at once distinguish one kind of food from another. It is impossible for us humans to conceive the intensity with which animals experience taste. Why, we would jump out of our chairs if our food tasted as strongly to us as their food tastes to them! Our feeble taste for sugar can give us no notion of the joy a piece of sugar gives to a dog. This is because most animals have a very highly developed 'taste-brain'. Of this, too, man has only a tiny remnant left. Instead, he is able to form ideas; the 'taste-brain' has been metamorphosed so that he is able to form ideas.

Man has become the noblest being on the earth because only a tiny part of his brain is engaged in sense-perception; the rest of it has been transformed into an instrument of thinking and feeling. Thereby man becomes the highest being. So we can say that in the human brain a mighty transformation of the faculties of tasting and smelling has taken place and only tiny vestiges remain of the 'taste-brain' and the 'smell-brain'. In the animal, *this* [pointing to drawing] does not exist, but these faculties are very highly developed. The outer structures themselves are evidence of it. If man had a 'smell-brain' as highly developed as the dog's, he would have no forehead. The forehead would slope backward because the 'smell-brain' would have developed towards the back of the head. Since the 'smell-brain' is transformed, the forehead is lofty. The dog's nose stretches forward and its brain lies further back. Someone who trains himself to observe this can tell which kinds of animals have a particularly keen sense of smell. He needs only to observe whether the brain lies towards the back and the nose is highly developed; then he knows that this particular animal has a fine sense of smell.

Now let's look at the plants. Their noses continue right down to the root, down into the earth. Here, everything is nose, only — in contrast to man — this nose becomes aware of taste as well, of the world of taste. And you see, this shows us that man's higher development is due to the fact that these very faculties which the animals and plants possess are imperfect in him; they have been metamorphosed. So we can say that man is a being of greater perfection than the other creatures of nature because what is developed to perfection in them exists in him in an imperfect state!

You can easily understand this; just think of a chicken. It slips out of the shell and at once it can take care of its own needs; it can scratch about for its food straight away. Think of the human infant in comparison! The animal can do everything. Why? Because the organs of its brain have not yet been metamorphosed into organs of thinking. When a human being is born, his brain has to acquire mastery over these blunted remains of sense organs. And so a child has to learn, while the animal doesn't need to learn, for it knows everything from the start. Human beings, having one-sidedly developed only their brain, can think with great subtlety but are terribly clumsy fellows. It is important for the human being that not too much of his brain should be transformed. If too much has been transformed, he may be a good poet but he will certainly not be a good mechanic. He will have no knack for doing things in the outside world.

This state of things is connected with what I was talking about the other day, when I said that many people, owing to excessive consumption of potatoes, have transformed a very large part of their brain. The result is that such people are clever but unskilful. That is so often true today. They have to struggle to do things that they should really be able to do quite easily. For instance, there are people who are quite unable to sew on a trouser-button. They are able to write a marvellously good book, but they are incapable of sewing on a button! This is because the nerves which are nerves of perception in the more delicate organs have been transformed almost entirely into brain-nerves.

Once I knew a man who had a terrible dread of the future.[17] He argued that in olden times man's senses were more delicate, more keen, just because he had less brain, and that in the course of human evolution what had in earlier times belonged to the senses and enhanced their perception was metamorphosed into a clever brain. The man was afraid that this would go further, that more and more of the sensory brain would become thinking brain, so that finally human beings would be utterly incapacitated, going about with defective eyes and so forth. In olden times people went through life with good sight; now they need glasses. Their sense of smell is not nearly as keen as it was once. Their hands are becoming clumsy. And anything that becomes clumsy is bound to deteriorate. This man was afraid that everything would be transformed into brain and that the human head would get bigger and bigger and the legs smaller and smaller and all would atrophy. He thought quite seriously that human beings would someday be no more than round heads rolling around the world – and then what would happen? The man was in absolute, grave earnest.

And his idea was perfectly correct. For if the human being does not find his way again to what he was once able to grasp through imagination, if he does not return to the spirit, then he will indeed become a round sphere of this kind! It is literally true that spiritual science does not simply make us clever. As a matter of fact, if we take it merely as one more theory, far from becoming more clever, we will become definitely more stupid. But if we assimilate spiritual science in the right way, it will work into our very fingers! Clumsy fingers will become more skilful again because the external world is getting its rightful significance again. Through spiritual science the outer world becomes spiritualized, but that does not make you clumsier. These are things to which attention must be paid.

You see, in the days when mankind created sagas, legends, mythologies (there was recently a question about this), much less sense activity had so far been transformed into brain. In those days, people dreamed more than we do now, and when they dreamed, pictures appeared to them. Our thoughts today are barren. And the stories you hear about Wotan, Loki, about the old Greek gods – Zeus, Aphrodite and so forth – these stories originated from the fact that man did not yet have so much of that cleverness which is valued so highly today. People become more clever, certainly—but one learns to know the world not merely through intelligence but rather by learning to observe it.

Think of an adult person with a child before him. The adult may be a bit conceited about his own cleverness; if so, the child will seem stupid. But if the adult has any sense for what comes from a child's very nature, he will regard that as having far higher value than his own cleverness. One cannot grasp what exists in nature by brainwork alone, but by being able to penetrate into the secrets of nature. Cleverness does not necessarily lead to knowledge. A clever man is not necessarily very wise. Clever people can't, of course, be stupid, but they may certainly lack wisdom; they may have no real knowledge of the world. Cleverness can be used in all sorts of ways: to classify plants and minerals, to make chemical compounds, to vote, to play dominoes and chess, to speculate on the Stock Exchange. The cleverness by which people cheat on the Stock Exchange is the same cleverness that one uses to study chemistry. The only difference is that a person is simply concentrating on something else when studying chemistry than when speculating on the Stock Exchange! Cleverness is present in both cases. It is simply a question of what one is concentrating on.

Obviously, too much should not be transformed into brain. If one were to dissect the heads of great financial magnates, one would find extraordinary brains. In this area, anatomy has brought a great deal to light. It has been possible to see proof of cleverness in a brain—but never proof of knowledge!

So, I have tried to develop a few aspects of the question. I hope you are not altogether dissatisfied with the answer. As soon as I return, we will have the next meeting. I'm sorry I can't give lectures here and in England at the same time—

such a thing is still beyond us! When we reach that point, there will be no need for a pause. But for the time being, gentlemen, I must say goodbye.

The planetary influences on animals, plants and rocks

Rudolf Steiner: Good morning, gentlemen! Are there any questions?

Written question: Mars is near the earth. What effect does that have upon the earth? What is known about Mars?

Rudolf Steiner: There has been a great deal of talk recently about the proximity of Mars to the earth, and the newspapers have made utterly futile statements without even a rudimentary understanding of what this means. We must not attach prime importance to external planetary constellations due to the relative positions of earth and sun, because the influences arising from them do not really amount to very much. It is interesting that there has been all this talk about the proximity of Mars, because every planet, including the moon, is constantly coming nearer to the earth, and the planets are undergoing a process that will finally end in all of them uniting again with the earth, forming a single body.

Of course, if it is imagined, as most people imagine today, that the planets are solid bodies just like the earth, the expectation could well be that if they were to unite with the earth this would mean the end of all life on our globe! But no such thing will happen, because the degrees of density of the various planets are not the same as that of the earth. If Mars, for instance, were actually to descend and unite with the earth, it would not be able to lay waste the land but only to inundate it. For as far as investigation is possible — it can never be done with physical instruments but only through spiritual science, spiritual vision — Mars consists primarily of a more or less fluid mass, not as fluid as our water but, shall we say, more like the consistency of jelly, or something of that kind. There are also dense components, but they are not as densely solid as those of our earth. Their consistency would be more comparable to that of the antlers or horns of our animals, which form out of the general mass and dissolve back into it again. So we must realize that the constitution of Mars is entirely different from that of our earth.[18]

Now a great deal is said about 'canals' existing on Mars. But why 'canals'? There is nothing to be seen except lines, and these are called canals.[19] In one sense that is correct, but in another, incorrect. As Mars is not solid to the degree that the earth is solid, one cannot, of course, speak of canals as we know them on the earth. But it can be said that on Mars there is something rather similar to our trade winds. You know that the warm air from the Torrid Zone of the earth, from Africa, streams towards the cold North Pole, and the air from the cold North Pole streams back towards the central region of the earth. So that if looked at from outside, such lines would indeed be seen, but they are the lines of the trade winds, of the air currents in the trade winds. There is something rather similar on Mars. Only everything on Mars is much more full of life than on the earth. The earth is a dead planet in a far stronger sense than Mars, on which everything is still more or less living.

I want to mention something that can help you to understand the character of Mars' relation to the earth. We know that the sun, to us the most important of all the heavenly bodies, sustains a very great deal on the earth. Think of the sun as we know it from day to day. At night you see the plants drawing in their blossoms because the sun is not shining on them. By day they open again to the sun's rays. Very many things depend upon the spread of sunlight over one part of the earth and the spread of darkness over another part when the sun is not there. But if you think of a whole year, you could not conceive of the plants growing in the spring if the sun's power did not return. Again, when the sun loses power in the autumn, the plants fade away, all life dies and snow falls.

Quite obviously, life on the earth is connected with the sun. Indeed, we humans would be unable to breathe the air around us if the sun were not there, if the rays of the sun did not make the air suitable for us to breathe. The sun is undeniably the most important heavenly body for us. Just think what a different story it would be if the sun were not—as it appears—to go around the earth every 24 hours but instead took twice that time! All life would be slower. So all life on earth depends upon the revolution of the sun around the earth. In reality, of course, the sun does not revolve around the earth, but that is how it appears.

The influence of the moon is of less significance for man, but nevertheless it is there. When you remember that the tides ebb and flow according to the moon, that they have the same rhythm as the moon's revolution, you will realize with what kind of power the moon works upon the earth. And then it will also be clear that the time of the moon's rotation around the earth has a definite significance. If you were to investigate how the plants develop when the sun has shone upon them, you would also find evidence of the influence of the moon. Thus the sun and the moon have a tremendous influence upon the earth. We can recognize the lunar influence from its rotation period, that is, from the time it takes for the moon to become full moon, new moon, and so on. We can recognize the influence of the sun from its rising and setting, or from the fact that it acquires its power in the spring and loses it in the autumn.

And now let me tell you something. You all know of the existence of the grubs of cockchafers. These little wormlike creatures are particularly harmful when they eat up our potatoes. There are years when the potatoes are unharmed by these troublesome little maggots, and then there are years when simply nothing can be done because the grubs are everywhere at work. Well now, suppose there has been a year when the grubs have eaten nearly all the potatoes — and if you wait for another four years, the cockchafers will be there in great numbers, because it takes them four years to develop from the grubs. There is a period of approximately four years between the appearance of the grubs, which, like all insects, first have a maggot form before becoming a chrysalis, and the fully developed insect. The grub needs four years to develop into the cockchafer. Naturally, there are always cockchafers, but if there are only a few grubs some year, four years after that there will only be a few cockchafers. The number of cockchafers depends upon the number of grubs that were present four years earlier.

We can see quite clearly that this period of time is connected with the rotation of Mars. The course of propagation of certain insects shows us the kind of influence that Mars exercises upon the life of the earth. But the influence is rather hidden. The influence of the sun is quite obvious, that of the moon not obvious to the same extent, and the influence of Mars is hidden. Everything for which intervals of years are needed on the earth — as in the case of grubs and cockchafers — is dependent upon Mars. So there you see a significant effect of Mars.

Of course someone may say that he doesn't believe this. Well, gentlemen, we ourselves can't possibly undertake all the necessary experiments, but anyone who doesn't believe what I've said should do the following. He should take the grubs he has collected in a year when they are very numerous and force their development artificially in some container. Within the same year he will find that the majority of them do not develop into cockchafers. Such experiments are never carried out because people do not believe such things.

However, we come now to the essential point. The sun has the most powerful influence of all. But it exerts its greatest influence upon everything on the earth that is dead, that must be awakened to new life every year—while the moon influences only what is living. Mars exerts its influence only upon what exists in a more delicate form of life, in the sentient realm. The other planets exert influence on what is of the nature of soul and spirit. The sun, then, is the heavenly body that works most strongly; it works into the very minerals of the earth. In the minerals the moon can do nothing—nor Mars. If the moon were not there, no animal creature could live and move about on the earth; there could only be plants on the earth, no animals. Again, there are many animal creatures that could not have intervals of years between the larva-stage and the insect if Mars were not there. You see how closely all things are connected.

For instance, we might ask ourselves: When do we human beings become fully grown? When does the process of our development stop? Obviously very early, at the age of about 20 or 21. And yet even then something continues to develop. Most people do not actually grow any more, but something develops inwardly. Until about our thirtieth year we do really 'increase'; but then, for the first time, we begin to 'decrease'. If we compare this with occurrences in the universe, we get the rotation period of Saturn.

Thus the planets exercise their influence upon more delicate conditions of growth and of life. So when, like all the planets, Mars comes near the earth, we must not attach primary importance to this external proximity. What is of far greater importance is how things in the universe are connected with finer, more delicate states and conditions of life.

You must remember that the constitution of Mars is quite different from that of the earth. As I said, Mars is not densely solid in the sense in which the earth is solid today. But I described to you quite recently how the earth too was once in a condition when mineral, solid matter took shape for the first time, how there were then gigantic animals which, however, had no solid bones as yet. Mars today is in a condition similar to that of the earth in that earlier epoch and therefore also has upon it those living beings, those animal beings which the earth had upon it at that time. And 'human beings' on Mars are as they were on the earth at that time—still without bones. I described this to you when I was speaking of an earlier period of the earth. These things can be known. They cannot become known by the means employed in modern science for acquiring knowledge; nevertheless it is possible to know these things. If, then, you want to have an idea of what Mars is like today, picture to yourselves what the earth was like in a much earlier age—then you will have a picture of Mars.

You know that on the earth today the trade winds blow from the south to the north, from the north to the south. These streams were once much denser than the air. They were currents of fluid, watery air; so it is on Mars today. The air currents on Mars are much more full of life, much more watery.

Jupiter consists almost entirely of air, but again somewhat denser than the air of the earth. Jupiter today represents a condition towards which the earth is now striving, which it will attain only in the future.

And so in the planetary system we find certain states or conditions through which the earth also passes. When we understand the planets in this sense, we understand them rightly.

Has anyone something else to ask about this subject? Perhaps Herr Burle himself?

Herr Burle: I am quite satisfied, thank you!

Question: In one of your last lectures you said that the scents of flowers are related to the planets. Does this also apply to the colours of flowers and colours of stones?

Rudolf Steiner: I will repeat very briefly what I said. It was also in answer to a question that had been asked. I said that flowers, and also other substances of the earth, have scent — something in them that exercises a corresponding influence upon man's organ of smell. I said that this is connected with the planets, that the plants and, similarly, certain substances, are 'big noses', noses that perceive the effects coming from the planets. The planets have an influence upon life in its finer, more delicate forms — here, once again, we must think of the finer forms of life. And it can be said that the plants really do come into being out of the scent of the universe, but this scent is so rarefied, so delicate, that we human beings with our coarse noses do not smell it.

But I reminded you that there can be a sense of smell quite different from that possessed by man. You need think only of police dogs. A thief has stolen something and the police dog is taken to the spot where the theft has been committed; he picks up the scent, then leads the police on the trail and the thief is often found. Police dogs are used in this way. All kinds of interesting things would come to light if one were to study how scents that are quite imperceptible to a human being are perceptible to a dog.

People have not always realized that dogs have such keen noses. If they had, dogs would have been used sooner to assist the police. It is only rather recently that this has been discovered. Likewise, people today still have no conception of what indescribably delicate noses are possessed by the plants. As a matter of fact, the entire plant is a nose; it takes in the scent of the universe, and if its structure is such that it gives back this cosmic aroma in the way that an echo gives back a sound, it becomes a fragrant plant. So we can say that the scents of flowers, of plants in general, and also other scents on the earth, do indeed relate to the planetary system.

The question has now been raised as to whether this also applies to the colours of plants and flowers. As I said, the plant takes shape out of the aroma of the universe and throughout the year it is exposed to the sun. While the form of the plant is shaped by the planets out of cosmic fragrance, its colour is due to the sun and also to some extent to the moon. The scent and the colour of plants do not, therefore, come from the same source; the scent comes from the planets, the colour from the sun and moon. Things don't always have to come from the same source; just as one has a father and a mother, so the plant has its scent from the planets and its colour from the sun and moon.

You can see from the following that the colours of plants are connected with the sun and moon. If you take plants that have beautiful green leaves and put them in the cellar, they become white, they lose every trace of colour because the sun has not been shining on them. They retain their structure, their form, because cosmic fragrance penetrates everywhere, but they don't keep their colour because no sunlight reaches them. The colours of the plants, therefore, undeniably come from the sun and, as I have said, also from the moon, only the latter is more difficult to determine. Experiments would have to be made and could be made, by exposing plants in various ways to moonlight; then one would certainly discover it.

Does anyone else want to say something?

Herr Burle: I would like to expand the question by asking about the colours of stones.

Rudolf Steiner: With stones and minerals it is like this. If you picture to yourself that the sun has a definite influence upon the plants every day, and also during the course of a year, then you find that the yearly effects of the sun are different from its daily effects. The daily effects of the sun do not bring about much change in the colour of the plants; but its yearly influence does affect their colour.

However, the sun not only has daily and yearly effects; it has other, quite different effects as well. I spoke to you about this some time ago, but I will mention it again.

Imagine the earth here. The sun rises at a certain point in the heavens, let us say in the spring, on the twenty-first of March. If in the present epoch we look at the point in the heavens where the sun rises on the twenty-first of March, we find behind the sun the constellation of the Fishes (Pisces). The sun has been rising in this particular constellation for hundreds of years, but always at a different point. The point at which the sun rises on the twenty-first of March is different every year. A year ago the sun rose at a point a little farther back, and still farther back the year before that. Going back through a few centuries we find that the point at which the sun rose in spring was still in the same constellation, but if we go back as far as AD 1200 we find that the sun rose in the constellation of the Ram (Aries). Again, for a long time it rose in spring in the constellation of the Ram. In still earlier ages, however, let us say in the epoch of ancient Egypt, the sun rose in the constellation of the Bull (Taurus), and before that in the constellation of the Twins (Gemini), and so on. So we can say that the point at which the sun rises in spring is changing all the time.

This indicates, as you can see, that the sun itself moves its position in the universe. I say it moves its position – but only apparently so, for in reality it is the earth that moves its position. That, however, does not concern us at the moment. In a period of 25,915 years, the point at which the sun rises in spring moves the whole way around the zodiac. In the present year – 1924 – the sun rises at a certain point in the heavens; 25,915 years ago, that is to say, 23,991 years before the birth of Christ (25,915 minus 1924) the sun rose at the same point! Since then it has made one complete circuit. The sun has a daily circuit, a yearly circuit, and a circuit that takes it 25,915 years to complete. Thus we have a sun-day, a sun-year and a great cosmic year consisting of 25,915 years.

That is very interesting, is it not? And the number 25,915 is itself very interesting! If you think of our breathing and remember that we take approximately 18 breaths a minute, you can reckon how many breaths we take in a day. Eighteen breaths a minute, 60 × 18 in an hour = 1080 breaths. How many breaths, then, do we take in a day, that is to say, in 24 hours? Twenty-four times 1080 = 25,920, which is approximately the same as this number 25,915! In a day, man breathes as many times as the sun needs years to make its circuit of the universe. These correspondences are very remarkable.

Now why am I telling you all this? You see, to give colour to a plant, the sun needs a year; to give colour to a stone, the sun needs 25,915 years. The stone is a much harder fellow. To bestow colour on a plant the sun makes a circuit lasting one year. But there is also a circuit which the sun needs 25,915 years to complete. And not until this great circuit has been completed is the sun able to give colour to the stones. But at any rate it is always the sun that gives the colour. You will realize from this how far removed the mineral kingdom is from the plant kingdom. If the sun did not move around yearly in the way it does, if it only made daily circuits as well as the great circuit of 25,915 years, then there would be no plants, and instead of cabbage you would be obliged to eat silica — and the human stomach would have to adjust itself accordingly!

Question: Do the herbs that grow on mountains have greater healing properties than those that grow in valleys? If so, what is the explanation?

Rudolf Steiner: It is an actual fact that mountain plants are more valuable as remedies than those that grow in valleys, particularly than those we plant in our ordinary gardens or in a field. It is a good thing that this is the case, for if the plants growing in the valleys were just like those on the mountains every foodstuff would at the same time be a medicine, and that would not do at all! The plants that have the greatest therapeutic value are indeed those that grow on the mountains. Why is this? All you need to do is to compare the kind of soil in which mountain plants grow with that in which valley plants grow.

It is a very different thing if plants grow wild, in uncultivated soil, or are artificially cultivated in a garden. Think of strawberries! Wild strawberries from the woods are tiny but very aromatic; garden strawberries have less scent, are less sharp in taste, but they can grow to an enormous size — why, there are cultivated strawberries as large as eggs! How is this to be accounted for? It is because the soil in the low-lying ground of valleys is not so full of stones that have crumbled away from the rock of the mountains. It is on mountains that really hard stone is to be found — the real mineral. Down in the valleys you find soil that has already been saturated and carried down by the rivers and is therefore completely pulverized. On the mountains there is also, of course, pulverized soil, but it is invariably permeated with tiny granules, especially, shall we say, of quartz, feldspar, and so on. Everywhere there are substances which can be used for healing. A very great deal can be achieved if, for example, we grind down quartz (silica) and make a remedy of it. We are then using these minerals directly as remedies.

The soil in low-lying valleys no longer contains these little stones. But on the mountains the stones continually crumble from the rocks, and the plants draw into their sap the tiny particles of these stones, and that makes them into medicinal plants.

Now the following is interesting. The so-called homoeopaths—they're not right about everything, but they're right about a good many things—these homoeopaths take substances and by grinding them finer and finer obtain medical remedies. If the substance were used in its crude state it would not be a remedy. But you see, the plants themselves are the most precious homoeopaths of all, for they absorb tiny, minute particles from all these stones, which otherwise would have to be refined and pulverized when a medicine is being prepared. So because nature does this far better than we could, we can take the plants themselves and use them directly for healing purposes. And it is a fact that the plants and herbs growing on mountains have far greater healing properties than those in the valleys.

You know, too, how the whole appearance of a plant changes. I spoke about the strawberry; the wild strawberry absorbs a large quantity of a certain mineral. Where does the wild strawberry thrive best? Where there are minerals that contain a little iron. This iron penetrates the soil and from that the strawberry gets its fragrant smell. Certain people whose blood is very sensitive get a rash when they eat strawberries. This is due to the fact that their blood in its ordinary state has sufficient iron and it is getting too much when they eat strawberries. If, then, some people with normal blood get a rash from eating strawberries, one can certainly advise someone whose blood is poor to eat them! In this way their medicinal value is gradually discovered. As a rule, the soil in gardens where giant strawberries grow contains no iron; there the strawberries propagate themselves without any impetus from iron. But people are rather short-sighted in this connection and don't follow things up over a sufficiently long period. It is a fact that by growing strawberries in soil that doesn't contain much iron one can get huge berries, for the reason that the plants do not become fully solid. For think of it—if the strawberry has to get hold of every tiny bit of iron there may be in the soil, then it must expand to the full! That is a characteristic of the strawberry.

Imagine some soil. It contains very minute traces of iron. The strawberry growing in the soil draws these traces of iron to itself from a long way off, for its root has a strong force and attracts the iron from some distance away. Now take a wild strawberry from the woods. It contains a very strong force. Put this strawberry into a garden; there is no iron in the soil, but the strawberry has acquired this tremendous force already, it has it within itself. It draws to itself everything it possibly can from a long way away, and nourishes itself exceedingly well. In a garden it does not get iron, but it draws everything else to itself because it is well able to do so. And so it becomes very large.

However, as I have said, people are very short-sighted; they do not observe things thoroughly. So they do not notice that although garden cultivation can produce huge strawberries for a number of years this will only last for a certain time. Then fertility dies away, and they must bring new strawberry plants from the woods. Fertility cannot be promoted entirely by artificial means; there must be knowledge of things that are directly connected with nature herself.

The rose is the best illustration of this. If you go out into the countryside you will see the wild rose, the dog rose, as it is called, *Rosa canina*. You know it, I'm sure. This wild rose has five rather pale petals. Why is it that it has this form, produces only five petals, remains so small and at once produces its fruit? These reddish rose-hips—you know them—develop from the wild rose. Well, this is due to the fact that the soil where the rose grows wild contains a certain kind of oil—just as the soil of the earth in general contains different oils in its minerals. We get oils from the earth or from the plants which have themselves absorbed them from the earth. Now the rose, when it is growing wild in the country, must seek far and wide with its roots in order to collect from the minerals the tiny amount of oil it needs in order to become a rose. Why is it that the rose must stretch out so far, must extend the drawing power contained in its root to such a distance? The reason is that there is very little humus in the country soil where the rose grows wild. Humus is more oily than the soil of the countryside. Now the rose has a tremendous power for drawing oil to itself.

When the rose is near soil which contains humus, this is fortunate for it; it draws a great deal of oil to itself and develops not only five petals but a whole mass of petals, becoming the luxuriantly petalled garden rose. But it no longer develops real rosehips because that would need what is contained in the stony soil out in the country. So we can make the wild rose into the ornamental garden rose when we transplant it into soil that is richer in humus, where it can easily get the oils from which to produce its many petals. This is the opposite of what happens with the strawberry; it is difficult for the strawberry to find in the garden what it finds out in the woods. The rose finds a great deal in the garden that is scarce in wild places and so it develops luxuriant petals; but its fruit formation is less developed.

So when we know what a particular soil contains, we know what will grow on it. Naturally, this is tremendously important for plant cultivation, especially for the plants needed in agriculture. For there, through manure and the substances added as fertilizers, the soil must be nourished and restored so that it will produce what is required. Knowledge of the soil is of enormous importance to the farmer. These things have been more or less forgotten. Simple country farmers used to apply the right manure by instinct. But nowadays in large-scale agriculture not much attention is paid to the matter. The consequence is that in the course of the last decades nearly all our foodstuffs have greatly deteriorated in quality from what they were when those of us who are now elderly were children.

Earlier this year there was an interesting agricultural conference at which farmers expressed their deep concern for what will become of the plants, of the foodstuffs, if this tendency continues. And indeed, gentlemen, it will continue! In the coming century foodstuffs will become quite unusable if a certain knowledge of the soil is not regained.

We have begun to approach agriculture through anthroposophical spiritual science. Recently I gave a course of lectures on agriculture near Breslau,[20] and an association has been formed that will take up this work. And we too have done something here to help the situation. We are only at the very beginning but the problem is being tackled. Thus anthroposophy will gradually penetrate into practical life.

There are still some sessions to make up, so let us meet again next Friday.[21]

The weather and its causes

Rudolf Steiner: Good morning, gentlemen! Does anyone have a question?

Question: Has Mars' proximity to the earth anything to do with the weather? The summer has been so unbelievably bad! Have planetary influences in general any effect upon the weather?

Rudolf Steiner: The weather conditions which have shown such irregularities through the years, particularly recent years, do have something to do with conditions in the heavens, but not specifically with Mars. When these irregularities are observed we must give our full attention to a phenomenon of which little account is usually taken, although it is constantly spoken of: I mean the phenomenon of sunspots. The sunspots are dark patches, varying in size and duration, which appear on the surface of the sun at intervals of about ten, eleven or twelve years. Naturally, these dark patches impede the sun's radiations, for, as you can well imagine, at the places where its surface is dark, the sun does not radiate. If in any given year the number of such dark patches increases, the sun's radiation is affected. And in view of the enormous significance the sun has for the earth, this is a matter of importance.

In another respect this phenomenon of sunspots is also noteworthy. In the course of centuries their number has increased, and the number varies from year to year. This is due to the fact that the position of the heavenly bodies changes as they revolve, and the aspect they present is therefore always changing. The sunspots do not appear at the same place every year, but — according to how the sun is turning—in the course of years they appear in that place again. In the course of centuries they have increased enormously in number and this certainly means something for the relationship of the earth to the sun.

Thousands of years ago there were no spots on the sun. They began to appear, they have increased in number, and they will continue to increase. Hence there will come a time when the sun will radiate less and less strongly, and finally, when it has become completely dark, it will cease to radiate any light at all. Therefore we have to reckon with the fact that in the course of time, a comparatively long time, the source of the light and life that now issues from the sun will be physically obliterated for the earth. And so the phenomenon of the sunspots—among other things—shows clearly that one can speak of the earth coming to an end. Everything of the earth that is spiritual will then take on a different form, just as I have told you that in olden times it had a different form. Just as a human being grows old and changes, so the sun and the whole planetary system will grow old and change.

The planet Mars, as I said, does not greatly influence weather conditions; Mars is more connected with phenomena that belong to the realm of life, such as the appearance and development of the grubs and cockchafers every four years. And please do not misunderstand this. You must not compare it directly with what astronomy calculates as being the period of revolution of Mars,[22] because the actual position of Mars comes into consideration here. Mars stands in the same position relative to the earth and the sun every four years, so that the grubs which take four years to develop into cockchafers are also connected with this. If you take two revolutions of Mars—requiring four years and three months—you get the period between the cockchafers and the grubs, and the other way around, between the grubs and the cockchafers. In connection with the smaller heavenly bodies you must think of the finer differentiations in earth phenomena, whereas the sun and moon are connected with cruder, more tangible phenomena such as weather, and so on.

A good or bad vintage year, for example, is connected with phenomena such as the sunspots, also with the appearance of comets. Only when observed in connection with phenomena in the heavens can occurrences on the earth be studied properly.

Now of course other matters must also be considered if one is looking for reasons for abnormal weather. For naturally the weather conditions, which concern us so closely because health and a great deal else is affected by them, depend upon very many factors. You must think of the following. Going back in the evolution of the earth we come to a time about six to ten thousand years ago. Six to ten thousand years ago there were no mountains in this region where we are now living. You would not have been able to climb the Swiss mountains then, because you would not have existed in the way you do now. You could not have lived here or in other European lands because at that time these regions were covered with ice. It was the so-called Ice Age. This Ice Age was responsible for the fact that the greatest part of the population then living in Europe either perished or was obliged to move to other regions. These Ice Age conditions will be repeated, in a somewhat different form, in about five, six or seven thousand years — not in exactly the same regions of the earth as formerly, but there will again be an Ice Age.

It must never be imagined that evolution proceeds in an unbroken line. To understand how the earth actually evolves we need to realize that interruptions such as the Ice Age do indeed take place in the ongoing course of evolution. What is the reason? The reason is that the earth's surface is constantly rising and sinking. If you go up a mountain which need by no means be very high, you will still find an Ice Age, even today, for the top is perpetually covered with snow and ice. If the mountain is high enough, it has snow and ice on it. But it is only when, in the course of a long time, the surface of the earth has risen to the height of a mountain that we can really speak of snow and ice on a very large scale. So it is, gentlemen! It happens. The surface of the earth rises and sinks. Some six thousand or more years ago the level of this region where we are now living was high; then it sank, but it is now already rising again, for the lowest point was reached around the year 1250. That was the lowest point. The temperature here then was extremely pleasant, much warmer than it is today. The earth's surface is now slowly rising, so that after five or six thousand years there will again be a kind of Ice Age.

From this you will realize that when weather conditions are observed over ten-year periods, they do not stay the same; the weather is changing all the time.

Now if in a given year a certain warm temperature prevails over regions of the earth, there are still other factors to be considered. Imagine the earth. At the Equator it is hot; above and below, at the Poles, it is cold. In the middle zone, the earth is warm. When people travel to Africa or India, they travel into the heat; when they travel to the North Pole or the South Pole, they travel into the cold. You certainly know this from accounts of polar expeditions.

Think of the distribution of heat and cold when you begin to heat a room. It doesn't get warm everywhere right away. If you got a stepladder and climbed to the top of it, you would find that down below it may still be quite cold while up above at the ceiling it is already warm. Why is that? It is because warm air, and every gaseous substance when it is warmed, becomes lighter and rises; cold air stays down below because it is heavier. Warmth always ascends. So in the middle zone of the earth the warm air is always rising.

But when it is up above it wafts towards the North Pole; winds blow from the middle zone of the earth towards the North Pole. These are warm winds, warm air. But the cold air at the North Pole tries to warm itself and streams downwards towards the empty spaces left in the middle zone. Cold air is perpetually streaming from the North Pole to the Equator, and warm air in the opposite direction, from the Equator to the North Pole. These are the currents called the trade winds. In a region such as ours they are not very noticeable, but very much so in others.

Not only the air, but the water of the sea, too, streams from the middle zone of the earth towards the North Pole and back again. That phenomenon is, naturally, distributed in the most manifold ways, but it is nevertheless there.

But now there are also electric currents in the universe; for when we generate electric wireless currents on the earth we are only imitating what is also present in some way in the universe. Suppose a current from the universe is present, let's say, here in Switzerland, where we have a certain temperature. If a current of this kind comes in such a way that it brings warmth with it, the temperature here rises a little. Thus the warmth on earth is also redistributed by currents from the universe. They too influence the weather.

In addition, however, you must consider that such electromagnetic currents in the universe are also influenced by the sunspots. Whenever the sun has spots, this gives rise to currents which affect the weather. These particular influences are of great importance.

Now in regard to the division of the seasons — spring, summer, autumn, winter — there is a certain regularity in the universe. We can indicate in our calendar that spring will begin at a definite time, and so on. This is regulated by the more obvious relationships in which the heavenly bodies stand to one another. But the influences resulting from this are few. Not many of the stars can be said to have an influence; most of them are far distant and their influence is only of a highly spiritual character.

But in regard to weather conditions the following may be said. Suppose you have a disc with, let's say, four colours on it — red, yellow, green, blue. If you rotate the disc slowly, you can easily distinguish all the four colours. If you rotate it more quickly, it is difficult but still possible to distinguish the colours. But if you rotate the disc very rapidly indeed, all the colours run into each other and you cannot possibly distinguish one from the other. Likewise, the seasons of spring, summer, autumn and winter can be distinguished because the determining factors are more or less obvious. But the weather depends upon so many circumstances that the mind cannot grasp all of them; it is impossible, therefore, to mark anything definite in the calendar in regard to it — while this is obviously quite possible in regard to the seasons. The weather is a complicated matter because so many factors are involved.

But in old folklore something was known about these things. Old folklore should not be cast aside altogether. When conditions of life were simpler, people took an interest in things far more than they do today. Today our interest in a subject lasts for 24 hours ... then the next newspaper comes and brings a new interest! We forget what happens — it is really so! The circumstances of our life are so terribly complicated. The lives of our grandparents, not to speak of our great-grandparents and great-great-grandparents, were quite different. They would sit together in a room around and behind the stove and tell stories, often stories of olden times. And they knew how the weather had been a long time ago, because they knew that it was connected with the stars; they observed a certain regularity in the weather. And among these great-grandparents there may have been one or two 'smart Alecs', as they are called. I mean someone who was a little more astute than the others, someone who had a certain cleverness. Such a person would talk in an interesting way. A 'smart Alec' might have said to a grandchild or great-grandchild: 'Look, there's the moon—the moon, you know, has an influence on the weather.' This was obvious to people in those days, and they also knew that rainwater is better for washing clothes than water fetched from the spring. So they put pails out to collect the rainwater to wash the clothes—my own mother used to do this. Rainwater has a different quality, it has much more life in it than ordinary water; it absorbs detergent and other additives far better. And it wouldn't be a bad idea if we ourselves did the same thing, for washing with hard water can, as you know, ruin your clothes.

So you see, these things used to be known; it was science in the nineteenth century that first caused people to have different views. Some of you already know the story I told once about the two professors at Leipzig University:[23] one was called Schleiden and the other Fechner. Fechner declared that the moon has an influence on the earth's weather. He had observed this and had compiled statistics on it. The other professor, Schleiden, was a very clever man. He said: 'That is sheer stupidity and superstition; there is no such influence.' Now when professors quarrel, nothing very much is gained by it and that's mostly the case when other people quarrel too! But both these professors were married; there was a Frau Professor Schleiden and a Frau Professor Fechner. In Leipzig at that time people still collected rainwater for washing clothes. So Professor Fechner said to his wife: 'That man Schleiden insists that one can get just as much rainwater at the time of new moon as at full moon. So let Frau Professor Schleiden put out her pail and collect the rainwater at the time of the next new moon, and you collect it at the time of full moon, when I maintain that you will get more rainwater.' Well, Frau Professor

Schleiden heard of this proposal and said: 'Oh no! I'll put my pail out when it is full moon and Frau Professor Fechner can put hers out at the time of new moon!' You see, the wives of the two professors actually needed the water! The husbands could squabble theoretically, but their wives worked on the basis of practical needs.

Our great-grandparents knew these things and told their grandchildren: 'The moon has an influence upon rainwater.' But everything connected with the moon is repeated every 18 or 19 years. For example, in a certain year, on a certain day, there are sun eclipses and on another day moon eclipses; this happens regularly in the course of 18 to 19 years. All phenomena connected with the positions of the stars in the heavens are repeated regularly. Why, then, should weather conditions not recur, since they depend upon the moon? After 18 or 19 years there must be something in the weather similar to what happened 18 or 19 years before. So as everything repeats itself, these people observed other repetitions too, and indicated in the calendar certain characteristics of the weather 18 or 19 years earlier, and now expected the same kind of weather after the lapse of this period. The only reason the calendar was called the Hundred Years' Calendar was that 100 is a number which is easy to keep in mind; other information was included in the calendar too, according to which predictions were made about the weather. Naturally, such things need not be quite exact, because conditions are complicated. Nevertheless, the predictions were useful, for people acted accordingly and did indeed succeed in producing better growing conditions. Through such observations something can certainly be done for the fertility of the soil. Weather conditions do depend upon the sun and moon, for the repetitions of the positions of the moon have to do with the relation of these two heavenly bodies.

In the case of the other stars and their relative positions, there are different periods of repetition. One such repetition is that of Venus, the morning and evening star. Suppose the sun is here and the earth over there. Between them is Venus. Venus moves to this point or that, and can be seen accordingly; but when Venus is here, it stands in front of the sun and covers part of it. This is called a 'Venus transit'.[24] (Venus, of course, looks much smaller than the moon, although it is, in fact, larger.) These Venus transits are very interesting because for one thing they take place only once every hundred years or so, and for another, very significant things can be observed when Venus is passing in front of the sun. One can see what the sun's halo looks like when Venus is passing in front of the sun. This event brings about great changes. Descriptions of it are very interesting. And as these Venus transits take place only once in about a hundred years, they are an example of phenomena about which science must admit that it believes some things that it has not actually perceived! If the scientists declare that they believe only things they have seen, an astronomer who was born, say, in the year 1890 could not lecture today about a Venus transit, for that has not occurred in the meantime, and presumably he will have died before the next Venus transit, which will apparently take place in the year 2004. In such cases even the scientist is obliged to believe in something he does not see!

Here again, when Venus is having a special effect upon the sun because it is shutting out the light, an influence is exercised upon weather conditions that occurs only once about every hundred years. There is something remarkable about these Venus transits and in earlier times they were regarded as being extraordinarily interesting.

Now when the moon is full, you see a shining orb in the sky; at other times you see part of a shining orb. But at new moon, if you train your eyes a little — I don't know whether you know this — you can even see the rest of the new moon.

If you look carefully when the moon is waxing, you can also see the other part of the moon—it appears bluish-black. Even at new moon a bluish-black disc can be seen by practised eyes; as a rule it is not noticed, but it can be seen. Why is it that this disc is visible at all? It is because the part of the moon that is otherwise dark is still illuminated by the earth. The moon is about 240,000 miles from the earth and is not, properly speaking, illuminated by it; but the tiny amount of light that falls upon the moon from the earth makes this part of the moon visible.

But no light at all radiates from the earth to Venus. Venus has to rely upon the light of the sun; no light streams to it from the earth. Venus is the morning and evening star. It changes just as the moon changes but not at the same rate. Yet the changes are not seen because Venus is very far away and all that is visible is a gleaming star. Looked at through a darkened telescope Venus can be seen to change, just as the moon changes. But in spite of the fact that Venus cannot be illuminated from the earth, part of it is always visible as a dull bluish light. The sun's light is seen on its upper hemisphere—but this is not the whole of Venus; where Venus is not being shone upon by the sun, a bluish light is seen.

Now, gentlemen, there are certain minerals—for instance, in Bologna—which contain barium compounds. Barium is a metallic element. If light is allowed to fall on these minerals for a certain time, and the room is then darkened, you see a bluish light shining from them. One says that the mineral, after it has been illuminated, becomes phosphorescent. It has caught the light, 'consumed' some of the light, and is now spitting it out again when the room is made dark. This is of course also happening before the room is darkened, but then the light is not visible to the eye. The mineral takes something in and gives something back. As it cannot take in a great deal, what it gives back is also not very much, and this is not seen when the room is light, just as a feeble candlelight is not seen in strong sunlight. But the mineral is phosphorescent, and if the room is darkened one sees the light it radiates.

From this you will certainly be able to understand where the light of Venus comes from. While it receives no light from this side, Venus is illuminated from the other side by the sun, and it eats up the sun's light, so to say. Then, when you see it on a dark night, it is expelling the light, it becomes phosphorescent. In days when people had better eyes than they have now, they saw the phosphorescence of Venus. Their eyes were really better in those days; it was in the sixteenth century that spectacles first began to be used, and they would certainly have come earlier if people had needed them! Inventions and discoveries always come when they are needed by human beings. And so in earlier times the changes that come about when phosphorescent Venus is in transit across the sun were also seen. And in still earlier times the conclusion was drawn that because the sun's light is influenced at that time by Venus, this same influence will be there again after about a hundred years; and so there will be similar weather conditions again in a region where a transit of Venus is seen to take place. (As you know, eclipses of the sun are not visible everywhere, but only in certain regions.) In a hundred years, therefore, the same weather conditions will recur—so people concluded—and they drew up the Hundred Years' Calendar accordingly.

Later on, people who did not understand the thing at all made a Hundred Years' Calendar every year, and then found that the details given in the calendar did not tally with actual facts. The calendar could just as well have said: 'If the cock crows on the dunghill, the weather either changes, or stays as it is!' But originally, the principle of the thing was perfectly correct. People perceived that when

Venus transits the sun, this produces weather conditions that are repeated somewhere after a hundred years.

Since the weather of the whole year is affected, then the influences are at work not only during the few days when Venus is in transit across the sun but they last for a longer period. So you see from what I have said that to know by what laws the weather is governed on a particular week or day one would have to ask many questions. How many years ago was there a Venus transit? How many years ago was there a sun eclipse? What is the present phase of the moon? I have mentioned only a few points. One would have to know how the trade winds are affected by magnetism and electricity, and so on. All these questions would have to be answered if one wanted to determine the regularity of weather conditions. It is a never-ending subject! People will eventually give up trying to make definite predictions about the weather. Although we hear about the regularity of all the phenomena with which astronomy is concerned—astronomy, as you know, is the science of the stars—the science that deals with factors influencing the weather (meteorology, as it is called) is by no means definite or certain. If you get hold of a book on meteorology, you'll be exasperated. You'll exclaim that it's useless, because everyone says something different. That is not the case with astronomy.

I have now given you a brief survey of the laws affecting wind and weather and the like. But it must still be added that forces arising in the atmosphere itself have a tremendously strong influence on the weather. Think of a very hot summer when lightning constantly flashes from the clouds and thunder continually rumbles; there you have influences on the weather that come from the immediate vicinity of the earth. Modern science holds a strange view of this. It says that it is electricity that causes lightning to flash out of the clouds. Now you probably know that electricity is explained to children at school by rubbing a glass rod with a piece of cloth smeared with some kind of amalgam; after it has been rubbed for some time, the rod begins to attract little scraps of paper, and after still more rubbing, sparks are emitted, and so on. Such experiments with electricity are done in school, but care has to be taken to wipe everything thoroughly beforehand, because the objects that are to become electric must not even be moist, let alone wet; they must be absolutely dry, even warm and dry, for otherwise nothing will come from the glass rod or the stick of sealing-wax. From this you can gather that electricity is conducted away by water and fluids. Everyone knows this, and naturally the scientists know it, for it is they who do the experiments. In spite of this, however, they declare that lightning comes out of the clouds — and clouds are certainly wet!

If it were a fact that lightning comes out of the clouds, 'someone' would have had to rub them long enough with a gigantic towel to make them quite dry! But the matter is not so simple. A stick of sealing-wax is rubbed and electricity comes out of it; and so the clouds rub against one another and electricity comes out of them! But if the sealing-wax is just slightly damp, electricity does not come out of it. And yet electricity is alleged to come out of the clouds — which are all moisture! This shows you what kind of nonsense is taught nowadays. The fact of the matter is this. You can heat air and it becomes hotter and hotter. Suppose you have this air in a closed container. The hotter you make the air, the greater is the pressure it exerts against the walls of the container. The hotter you make it, the sooner it reaches the point where, if the walls of the container are not strong enough, the hot air will burst them asunder. What's the usual reason for a child's balloon bursting? It's because the air explodes from it. Now when the air becomes hot it acquires the density, the strength to burst. The lightning process originates in the vicinity of the earth; when the air gets hotter and hotter, it becomes strong enough to burst. At very high levels the air may for some reason become intensely hot — this can happen, for example, as the result of certain influences in winter when somewhere or other the air has been very strongly compressed. This intense heat will press out in all directions, just as hot air will press against the sides of a container. But suppose you have a layer of warm air, and there is a current of wind sweeping away the air. The hot air streams towards the area where the air is thinnest.

Lightning is the heat generated in the air itself that makes its way to where there is a kind of hole in the surrounding air, because at that spot the air is thinnest. So we must say: Lightning is not caused by electricity, but by the fact that the air is getting rid of, emptying away, its own heat.

Because of this intensely violent movement, the electric currents that are always present in the air receive a stimulus. It is lightning that stimulates electricity; lightning itself is not electricity.

All this shows you that warmth is differently distributed everywhere in the air; this again influences the weather. These are influences that come from the vicinity of the earth and operate there.

You will realize now how many things influence the weather and that today there are still no correct views about these influences — I have told you about the entirely distorted views that are held about lightning. A change must come about in this domain, for spiritual science, anthroposophy, surveys a much wider field and makes thinking more mobile.

We cannot, of course, expect the following to be verified in autopsies, but if one investigates using spiritual scientific methods, one finds that in the last hundred years human brains have become much stiffer, alarmingly stiffer, than they were formerly. One finds, for example, that the ancient Egyptians thought quite definite things, of which they were just as sure as we ourselves are sure of the things we think about. But today we are less able to understand things in the winter than in the summer. People pay no attention to such matters. If they would adjust themselves to the laws prevailing in the world, they would arrange life differently. In school, for instance, different subjects would be studied in the winter than in the summer. (This is already being done to some extent in the Waldorf School.[25]) It is not simply a matter of taking botany in the summer because the plants bloom then, but some of the subjects that are easier should be transferred to the winter, and some that are more difficult to the spring and autumn, because the power to understand depends upon this. It is because our brains are harder than human brains were in former times. What we can think about in a real sense only in summer, the ancient Egyptians were able to think about all year round. Such things can be discovered when one observes the various matters connected with the seasons of the year and the weather.

Is there anything that is not clear? Are you satisfied with what has been said? I have answered the question at some length. The world is a living whole and in explaining one thing one is naturally led to other things, because everything is related.

Question: Herr Burle says that his friends may laugh at his question—he had mentioned the subject two or three years ago. He would like to know whether there is any truth in the saying that when sugar is put into a cup of coffee and it dissolves properly, there will be fine weather, and when it does not dissolve properly there will be bad weather.

Rudolf Steiner: I have never done this experiment, so I don't know whether there is anything in it or not. But the fact of the sugar dissolving evenly or unevenly might indicate something—if, that is to say, there is anything in the state-ment at all. I speak quite hypothetically, because I don't know whether there is any truth in it, but we will presume that there is.

There is something else that certainly has some sig-nificance, for I have observed it myself. What the weather is likely to be can be discovered by watching tree frogs, green tree frogs. I've made tiny ladders and observed whether they ran up or down. The tree frog is very sensitive to what the weather is going to be. This need not surprise you, for in certain places it has happened that animals in their stalls suddenly became restless and tried to get out; those that were not tethered ran away quickly. Human beings stayed where they were. And then there was an earthquake! The animals knew it beforehand, because something was already happening in nature in advance. Human beings with their crude noses and other crude senses do not detect anything, but animals do. So naturally the tree frog, too, has a definite 'nose' for what is coming. The word *Witterung* [weather] is used in such a connection because it means 'smelling' the weather that is coming.*

Now there are many things in the human being of which he himself has no inkling. He simply does not observe them. When we get out of bed on a fine summer day and look out the window, our mood is quite different from when a storm is raging. We don't notice that this feeling penetrates to the tips of our fingers. What the animals sense, we also sense; it is only that we don't bring it to our con-sciousness.

So just suppose, Herr Burle, that although you know nothing about it, your fingertips, like the tree frogs, have a delicate feeling for the kind of weather that is coming. On a

---

*In English we have the expression 'to get wind of something'. (Trans-lator's note)

day when the weather is obviously going to be fine and you are therefore in a good mood, you put the sugar into your coffee with a stronger movement than on another day. So the way the sugar dissolves does not necessarily depend upon the coffee or the sugar, but upon a force that is in yourself. The force I'm speaking of lies in your fingertips themselves; it is not the conscious force that is connected with you putting sugar into the coffee. It lies in your fingertips, and is not the same on a day when the weather is going to be fine as when the weather is going to be bad. So the dissolving of the sugar does not depend upon the way you consciously put it into your coffee but upon the feeling in your fingertips, upon how your fingertips are 'sensing' the weather. This force in your fingertips is not the same as the force you are consciously using when you put sugar into your coffee. It is a different force, a different movement.

Think of the following. A group of people sits around a table; sentimental music, or perhaps the singing of a hymn, puts them into a suitable mood. Then delicate vibrations begin to stir in them. Music continues. The people begin to convey their vibrations to the table, and the table begins to dance. This is what may happen at a spiritualistic séance. Movements are set going as the effect of the delicate vibrations produced through the music and the singing. In a similar fashion the weather may also cause very subtle movements, and these in turn may influence what happens with the sugar in the coffee. But I am speaking quite hypothetically because, as I said, I don't know whether it is absolutely correct in the case you are speaking of. It is more probable that it is a premonition which the person himself has about the weather that affects the sugar—although this is not very probable either. I am saying all this as pure hypothesis.

A spiritual scientist has to reject such phenomena until he possesses strict proof of their validity. If I were to tell you in a casual way the things I do tell you, you really wouldn't have to believe any of it. You should only believe me because you know that things which cannot be proved are not accepted by spiritual science. And so as a spiritual scientist I can only accept the story of the coffee if it is definitely proved. In the meantime I can make the comment that one knows, for instance, of the delicate vibrations of the nerves, also that this is how animals know beforehand of some impending event — how even the tree frog begins to tremble and then the leaves on which it sits also begin to tremble. So it could also be — I don't say that it is, but it could be — that when bad weather is coming, the coffee begins to behave differently from the way it behaves when the weather is good.

So — let us meet next Wednesday.[26] After that, I think we'll be able to return to regular sessions.

Form and origin of the earth and moon — causes of volcanic activity

Rudolf Steiner: Good morning, gentlemen! Perhaps someone has a question?

Question: Why does lightning not come in a straight line, instead of zigzag? Should it not take a straight line?

Rudolf Steiner: So, the questioner thinks that when lightning is released from the air, as I described last time, it ought to come in a straight line. But it takes a zigzag form and can that be explained? Yes, one can indeed explain it.

Let us consider again the explanation I gave of how lightning actually comes about. I told you that lightning arises from overheated air, the overheated universe, overheated cosmic gas. I said that there is no question of lightning arising from some sort of friction of the clouds. Clouds, of course, are wet, and if you want to produce miniature lightning with laboratory apparatus, everything must first be wiped absolutely dry. It must not be supposed, therefore, that lightning is a true electrical phenomenon that comes about from the friction of dry elements. It is known that when one rubs glass or sealing wax one produces electricity and so people think that if clouds rub together — well, then there'll be electricity there too. But that is not so. What happens is this. As a consequence of the inner overheating of the cosmic gas, the warmth living in the cosmic gas comes out in the way I have described. Through the fact that the air exerts less pressure on one side or another, the radiation of the overheated force goes towards that side and lightning flashes.

Now let us imagine that we have this happening some-

where. In consequence of greatly overheated cosmic gas —
not clouds — the lightning flashes out. And it is quite correct
to think that it should stream out in a straight line.

But you see, it is like this. Picture to yourselves: if an
accumulation of heat is present somewhere, it is generally
not alone; there are similar accumulations in the neighbourhood. In fact, if the earth is here, let us say, and one
looks up there and lightning begins where a concentration
of heat exists, then in the neighbourhood there are other
accumulations — they are not all at one single place. You can
imagine, of course, that these accumulations of heat are
connected with the sun's radiations at various places. Now
there are these heat accumulations along the entire path of
the lightning and while it is streaming out it snatches up
these other accumulations in its course. So it shines here,
then over there, and so on. It takes all the other accumulations with it, and so it moves quite irregularly, and gets this
seemingly zigzag formation. The lower it descends, the
more it does move in a straight line. There are no longer
these heat accumulations; they were higher up. The zigzag
of the lightning comes about because it does not arise in one
single spot, but from where the heat accumulations are
strongest and then it carries the others along on its way.
That's similar to when you're out walking and you meet an
acquaintance and take him along with you, then the two of
you pick up another one, and so on. So that's the story of the
lightning.

Now perhaps someone has another question?

Question: Could we hear something about the origin of
volcanoes?

Rudolf Steiner: That's a question that can't be answered quite
so quickly. I will lead you to the point where you can find an
answer to it. For if you read modern books you can certainly
find all sorts of ideas on the origin of volcanoes, but if you
read older books, lying farther back in time, you find other

views, and in still earlier books again other views. People have never enquired into the real origin of the earth and so views on volcanic phenomena have changed in the course of time. As a matter of fact, no one has been able to form a true idea of how these fire-erupting mountains originated.

One must go very far back if one wants to understand this. Otherwise one cannot grasp how it happens that at certain spots on the earth fiery, molten masses erupt. One will be able to form an idea of it only if one first of all rejects the dictum that the earth was once a balloon of gas, that it became more and more solid, and that there is fire in the interior which for some reason or other erupts here or there. That is a convenient explanation, but it brings us no nearer to an understanding.

I'll tell you a little story. It's a long time ago, more than forty years, that we did a certain experiment in the laboratory of the geologist Hochstetter[27] of Vienna. He is long since dead. We produced a substance that contained — among other things — a little sulphur. We didn't put it all together, but this is what we did: here someone had a bit of the stuff, there someone had a bit, over there a bit, and so on, and we hurled, we shot the substance, all of us, towards a certain point. In this way there arose a little globe with all sorts of hills which was curiously like the moon seen through a telescope. Thus at that time in Hochstetter's geological laboratory an experiment was actually made by which a small moon was created. The surface of the moon as it is seen through a telescope had come out quite wonderfully. The whole thing looked just like a little moon. Above all one could see from this that a planetary body need not originate as gas, but can actually be flung together from all corners of the universe. Nor can we explain our earth in any other way than by its being thrown together out of the universe.

Now in connection with this I want to explain something

that is little spoken of today but which is nevertheless true. You hear it said everywhere, don't you, that the earth is a globe, has formed itself as a globe. Now actually it is not true that the earth is a globe! I will explain to you what the earth really is. It is only fantasy that the earth is a globe. If we picture the earth's true form as a regular solid, we come to what in science is called a tetrahedron. I will draw it for you, naturally only in perspective. A tetrahedron looks like this [see diagram].

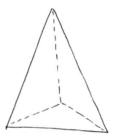

You see there are one, two, three triangles and here in front the fourth triangle. Can you picture it? It stands on a triangle, a triangle is underneath; and on that triangle, the base, are three other triangles; it forms a little pyramid. That is how we picture a tetrahedron. We must be clear that four triangles are joined to one another. We must stand it up on one triangle and the other three range upward like a pyramid. That is a perfectly regular solid.

But now imagine that I round out the surfaces of these triangles a little, then it becomes a little different. Now it stands on what has become rounded but yet is still free. And the sides of the triangles which formerly were straight lines are now rounded too. Can you picture that? So now there arises a form which is actually a tetrahedron become round! And you see, our earth is actually such a rounded tetrahedron.

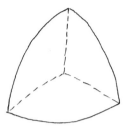

We can even find the edges, the sides of this earth tetrahedron. It is like this. Suppose I draw the earth as it is often drawn, on a flat plane — then here would be North America, here South America, between them, Central America. Over here we have Africa; here we have Europe. And there is Asia Minor, the Mediterranean, Greece, Italy, Spain, France, in fact Europe. Up here we have Scandinavia. There is England and over there is Asia. So we have Asia here, Africa here, Europe here and America here.

Now the South Pole is here, and around the South Pole in particular there are many volcanic mountains. There is the North Pole. And now it is like this. We can trace a line that goes from Central America, from the Colima volcano[28] down through the mountains that are called the Andes, down to the South Pole. It is a rounded edge. Then it goes on from the South Pole, goes over here past Africa to the volcanic mountains of the Caucasus. Then the same line comes over here, past Switzerland, over the Rhine and arrives there.

If you follow this line, which looks like a triangle, you can compare it with this triangle here. And so, if you take this portion of the earth, it is the base of a tetrahedron.

Just think, the base of a tetrahedron! Now, how do we come to that point there? Well, we have to go through to the other side of the earth. But I cannot draw that — I would have to make everything round. If I were to make it round, I would come to the point just over there in Japan. Thus if I

North Pole

South Pole

mark the tetrahedron, here we have Central America, here the South Pole, here the Caucasus, and over there, which one cannot see, would be Japan.

If we picture the earth in this way, we see that it exists in the universe as a rounded-out pyramid that sends its apex over there to Japan and has its base here, containing Africa, South America and the whole Southern Ocean. So the earth stands in the universe, curiously, as a rounded tetrahedron, as a kind of pyramid. That, gentlemen, is actually still the form of the earth!

And now if you take these lines that I've drawn forming the tetrahedron, you find that most of the volcanic moun-

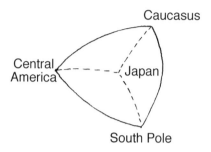

tains are located along the lines. There are frightful fire-belching mountains of which you've often heard, over in South America, in Chile and other places, then around the South Pole; and then there are the mighty ones in the Caucasus. And when you come over here, we don't have so many in our part of the continent, and yet it can be shown that there were once volcanoes here, but they are now extinct. For instance, when you drive along the stretch of road from northern Silesia to Breslau, you see a mountain standing conspicuously alone which people nowadays still fear. If you examine its rocks, you find this strange mountain standing there is simply an extinct volcano. Similarly we have extinct volcanoes in many parts of Germany.

And now let us continue. We have only marked out the base. Then we have lines everywhere that go towards Japan. Yes, and you see, along all these lines one would always be able to find volcanoes on the earth's surface! You can see that if someone sat down and drew the most important volcanoes, not on a flat surface, but so that they formed a solid, he would get this shape of the earth. Strangely, the volcanic mountains give us the lines that make the earth into a tetrahedron.

So now, if you do not picture the earth as originally a ball of gas which then became condensed — that's the convenient opinion which people hold — if you explain it as having been formed by substance flung from all sides, then

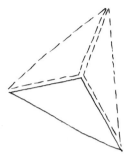

you must admit something else. If the earth is a tetrahedron, a regular solid, you'll have to explain it by imagining that a great master geometrician with plenty of knowledge had actually pushed the earth together from outside, along the lines which we still see today. Now imagine that I draw this tetrahedron, that I first fling this triangle in here from the periphery, then this triangle, then this, and then the one up above. I make it as small boys do: they cut out four triangles, tilt them together from outside and then glue them together to form a tetrahedron. And the earth too has originated like that; it has been flung together as triangles from outside.

Now watch such boys when they paste the triangles together; where they join the sides they must be careful to apply the paste or the glue evenly. As to the earth, at the places I've shown you — South America, then here towards the Caucasus and over here through the Alps, and so on — there the earth was originally 'cemented' together! But one finds when one examines the mountains that there it has, so to say, been joined rather badly; the sides don't quite fit together. If in particular we trace the line of mountains that passes from the Caucasus through our Carpathians and Alps, we can show from the form of the mountains that they have not yet quite grown together. The earth actually consists of four pieces flung out of cosmic space and joined together, four pieces which then form a tetrahedron, and along the edges there are still, as it were, places not tightly closed. At these leaky places it is possible for the cosmic heat from the sun to get into the earth more than at other places.

Now when the sun's power enters into these places beneath the surface of the earth, they become hotter and get soft — as is always the case when things, even metals, are consumed by fire — and they make an outlet for themselves seeking out those places which are not properly fastened together. Then through the combined cosmic action of the sun and the 'cemented' places of the earth there arise these regular volcanoes, the fire-belching mountains.

However, volcanoes are found at other places too. Etna, for instance, and Vesuvius do not, it is true, lie along these edges; where they are, no such line passes through. In fact, the very volcanoes that are not located along the principal lines are especially instructive, for one can learn from them what causes eruptions to occur.

You see, it can always be shown that when things like fiery eruptions happen on the earth, they are connected with the constellations, the relation of the stars to the sun. An eruption can never occur unless at some particular place the sun is able to shine more strongly than usual because it is not covered by other stars. If it is covered by other stars as is generally the case, then the sunshine is normal. Starlight is everywhere; one must not think that the stars are not up there during the day, it is just that we don't see them. In the old city of Jena where people had time to do such things, where so many German philosophers taught, where Haeckel[29] lived too, there is a deep cellar with a tower[30] above it, open at the top. If you go down into this cellar in the daytime and look up through the tower it is dark inside, but you see up above the most beautiful starry sky. When it is daytime, and clear and bright outside, you can see the most beautiful starlit heavens, with stars everywhere.

But when the stars are in such a position that the sun can develop its heat to full strength, when they do not obstruct the sun, then the sun's forces of warmth shine down upon some special places. These are the places where, after the earth had been fastened together, volcanoes later arose. They came about later. On the other hand, those that lie along the edges of the tetrahedron are the original volcanoes.

Now sometimes a person who is not actually a scientist by profession discovers quite useful things. Perhaps you've heard, or at least the older ones among you, of a certain Falb?[31] He was neither an astronomer nor a geologist nor geographer nor natural scientist, but a former priest who had given up his calling—run away from it! He devoted himself especially to a study of star constellations and whether they really have an influence on the earth. He came to the opinion that constellations are connected with volcanoes, that when the influence of the sun is supported by the stars in a certain way, a volcano erupts. He maintained further that floods also come about for the same reason, because water is attracted: beneath, the heated mass; above, the water.

But he did not stop there, claiming that in the mines the miners suffer most of all from so-called firedamp, that is, when the air in the mines catches fire by itself. He asked himself how this could happen. He decided that for this to happen the stars must aid the sun activity rather than opposing it. Then the force of the sun shines too strongly into the mine and the air in the mine ignites. Therefore, said Falb, if one knows about mining conditions, one ought to be able to say when firedamp may be expected in the course of the year. So he made a calendar and indicated when, according to the constellations, firedamp must occur somewhere—so-called critical days.

This calendar has been printed many times with Falb's

critical days still recorded there. Now what was to be expected when these days arrived? Either the eruption of a volcano, or an earthquake (an earthquake is a subterranean tremor, subterranean overheating), or a flood, or firedamp. Now, gentlemen, I was present once at an amusing little incident. You see, this Falb was very clever, he had been able to light upon these facts, but he was also very conceited, frightfully conceited. As you know, to be learned is no protection from vanity. And the following happened. About 40 years ago I was at a lecture given by Falb. He went with great pompousness and a self-satisfied expression up to the podium and began his address. He said: 'Yes, this very day the stars are in a position from which one can deduce the occurrence of considerable firedamp.' At that moment the door opened and a messenger from the 'New Free Press' entered and handed him a telegram. Falb stood up there with his long patriarchal beard and said: 'It must be something important if they bring it to me in the lecture room!' He took out his knife and cut the telegram open and read: 'A terrible firedamp has occurred!' Now you can imagine the publicity he got! Falb had just said firedamp could happen today and the messenger brings the telegram! 'You see,' he said, 'proofs are laid on the table!' Those were his words. But the whole thing smelled of show business. Falb knew quite well that firedamp was due — that was correct. But he went early in the day to the office of the 'New Free Press' and left word that if such a telegram came, they should send it immediately to the lecture hall.

That is one of the tricks to which bad speakers gladly resort — though usually in a milder form! I am glad to relate the story so that audiences may be warned to be somewhat cautious and not simply accept everything. The clientele that Falb had at that time rustled with silk dresses and tuxedos; it was a very distinguished one. But you should have seen how impressed they were by his performance!

However strongly he might have voiced his opinion in words, the audience would never have been so convinced as they were by the entry at exactly the right moment of the messenger with the telegram. People would much rather be convinced by external events than by what can be expressed in words.

So one can say that at certain places, at the edges of this tetrahedron, the edges of the earth are not completely sealed. It is therefore exposed to the cosmic warmth of sun and stars, and the consequence is that those lines of active volcanoes can be drawn. Outbursts of volcanic fire can, of course, occur at other spots too.

But does this imply that the interior of the earth must necessarily be molten fire? That is what is constantly claimed. Actually there is no other proof of it than the fact that it becomes warmer and warmer the deeper one sinks a shaft into the earth. But one cannot go very deep. Moreover, with this increase of warmth as one descends into the earth there is likewise an increase of pressure. Whatever might be dissolved by the heat and become fluid is pressed together again by the pressure in the interior. If the earth were really molten inside then something else would not be true. One can consider, for instance, the weight of the earth. It is naturally hypothetical, since the earth floats freely in the universe and cannot be weighed. In order to weigh it, one would have to have it on top of another, gigantic earth, for if there is to be weight there must be something that attracts, that develops gravity. One could calculate how much it would weigh from how it attracts other bodies; in fact, such a calculation has been made. But if it were possible to weigh the earth one would find that it is far, far heavier than it would be if it were fluid inside. Goethe[32] for this reason vigorously attacked the idea that the interior of the earth was molten fire.

Now when one knows how the earth has been created,

when one sees that it is really an incompletely fastened tetrahedron, there is then no need to picture it as molten inside and to suppose that at certain times, one wouldn't know why or wherefore, it must suddenly erupt fire — like a moody, hysterical person! If the earth were molten inside, one would have to fancy that it is actually a little crazy — like someone who is insane and can at any moment begin to rage; one doesn't know when these moments will occur. But this is not true of the earth. You can always show where the warmth comes from, that it comes from outside, and that when such powerful heating occurs, not so very deep in the earth, then it forces an outlet for itself.

So the fire when Vesuvius or any other volcano erupts originates only when the temperature of the cosmos has become fiery. It always takes a little time before the effect is seen. The particular constellation of stars, for instance, must first work upon the earth for a time.

But that also follows from certain facts which I have already related here in quite a different connection. Imagine a part of the earth where the sun's rays strike powerfully, and underneath something develops that later seeks an outlet through an eruption or an earthquake.

You see, what I drew first, the powerful warmth going down into the earth; people don't feel that because they don't pay attention. At most, a few people at the place where there is not yet any hint of volcanic activity — though the effects of the sun's activity are already present in the air — have violent stomachaches, others have headaches, migraine, others find that their heartbeat is disturbed. But people put up with all that in a vague fashion and take no notice. But the animals, as I have said in another connection, which have more delicate noses, finer organs in this respect, perceive what is happening and leave if they can. The people, in spite of their stomachaches and headaches, don't know why the animals have become so restless and are running away. But after a few days the earthquake comes, or the volcanic eruption. The animals have fled because they already got wind of what was coming; human beings are so coarsely organized in this respect that they are not aware of the event until it arrives on their doorstep.

You can see from this that something is already happening a long time in advance before the final event takes place. What is happening is the streaming in of some cosmic heat. But you can still say that this cosmic heat only heats the ground, and where the earth contains substances that are easily inflammable, fire could of course ignite … but why, you may ask, should it all flare up instantly? Here I'll tell you something else. When one goes to Italy, to the places between Rome and Naples, particularly to the neighbourhood of Naples, and to the islands and peninsulas on the coast, the guides always delight in showing one the following experiment. They take a piece of paper and light it and hold it so — in a moment smoke begins to come out of the earth! The earth smokes — why? Because the air grows warm from the burning paper and so becomes lighter and expands. The warmth caused by the sun's heat streams out of the earth as smoke. This is very interesting to see. One lights a piece of paper and instantly the earth smokes at that spot.

Now think of that magnified to giant proportions, the sun heating not only the ground below, but also the air above — and you have Vesuvius. And when the latter has once established itself — well, then things have begun and the process continues in places that are especially favourable to it. It is interesting to realize that those very things that take place on earth irregularly, derive from the whole of cosmic space.

Now I told you that when we flung that sulphur substance in the geological laboratory, we produced something that really looked like a little moon. And so when one observes the real moon, which our little moon actually resembled, one gets the idea that it too has been flung together out of the universe. That is one idea one gets.

The other idea arises from spiritual scientific investigation, namely, that the moon was actually pushed out into the cosmos, largely from the earth. What does that mean? Well, we did that too in the laboratory. First we threw together a cosmic body from substances. Then we attacked it from all sides, flinging material against it from without, and lo and behold—it became more and more like a moon. And what has one got then? Well, one has the whole process. The main mass of the moon was cast out from the earth, and once it was there, fine matter from every part of space was flung against it. Fine matter is always present in the universe—it falls down in the meteors—it is always being flung out. And so one has the origin of the moon. These things are all connected.

The development of science, you know, is sometimes remarkable. A monument stands today in Heilbronn—certainly it is rather dreadful as a work of art, but still it stands there and represents Julius Robert Mayer.[33] If you hear about him in science today, you learn that he was a pioneering genius through his researches in the 1840s into the action of heat. Julius Robert Mayer was born in Heilbronn, practised there as a doctor and did not attract much attention. The scientists of the time paid no special attention to him. And although today he is generally well known as a highly gifted pioneer in physics, at that time when he sat for his medical examination at Tübingen he failed it. If you made investigations, you would come on the remarkable fact that the majority of people who later became geniuses failed their examinations at an earlier stage. And this was also the fate of Julius Robert Mayer. By the skin of his teeth he managed to scrape through and become a doctor. But no one considered him remarkable during his lifetime—in fact, quite the contrary. He became so enthusiastic about his discovery that he talked of it everywhere. Then people said that his mind was wandering and put him in an asylum. His own generation put him in a madhouse while posterity looks upon him as a great genius and puts up a monument to him in his native town.

It was Julius Robert Mayer who, after much thought and investigation, asked how it was that the sun which gives us so much heat does not become cold. He said to himself that it does not become as cold as it ought to become after continually giving out heat. He thought therefore that comets, an immense number of comets, must continually rush into the sun, hurled towards it from the universe. They are very fine, tenuous bodies, but they rush into it. It is true that they rush into the sun. The sun is very different from what the physicists of today imagine. They would be very astonished if they were to get near it; they would not find fiery gas but they would find something that causes any earthly substance to be sucked in and disappear. The sun is a vacuum that exerts suction. It is not a globe of gas. It resembles a pearl in the universe, a suction globe with nothing in it that one expects, but which continuously absorbs this mass of comets. The fine etheric structures of the universe, which are almost spiritual, are continuously being sucked in by the sun as nourishment. We still see today, therefore, this hurtling into the sun. This should draw our attention, gentlemen, to something important.

You see, when one arrives at the fact that the earth is really a tetrahedron—and if one has been obliged to study such forms and to note the number of sides and corners, one realizes that a certain knowledge of geometry is necessary to understand how to construct them—then one sees that they don't come about so simply. Boys enjoy doing it, making these tetrahedrons, cubes, octahedrons, icosahedrons, dodecahedrons, the five regular solids. They like to put them together from sheets of cardboard, gluing the pieces together, but one needs a knowledge of geometry to do this. Now the earth is formed in this very way out of the universe—formed from knowledge of geometry, in this sense, not formed through calculation, but with knowledge—for it is regular! You can infer from this that there is really geometry in the world, that everything is in harmony with geometry. That is true. Real science shows us something that I have always stated, namely that thoughts compose and are spread out through the world, thoughts are everywhere and only those people don't find them who have none themselves!

It is very praiseworthy, is it not, to be a free and independently thinking person? And yet it is slightly ridiculous to find the modern expression 'freethinker' which appeared in the nineteenth century. Thinking independently—that is very good, but many in their freedom have misused this expression 'freethinker'. And the people who felt themselves to be the freest thinkers were those who had the fewest thoughts, who simply repeated what other people had said. An Englishman made a delightful remark. He said, 'Free thought does not mean that people have thoughts, but that they are free from thought'—a remark that has been much quoted. What is a freethinker? A freethinker is one who is free from thinking! Well, in science one must endeavour not to develop such freedom from thought or else nothing will be achieved. The actual form of the earth could long ago have been discovered—the fact that it is not a completely spherical cabbage-head, but that it has something of the shape of a tetrahedron!

Knowledge of the earth is related to knowledge of man. Man imitates the universe in his own form. He copies the universe in his head, and so the head is round up above like the round universe. Below, where the jaws begin there are quite remarkable structures; they come from the triangular earth. In our jaw formation you find triangles everywhere, they come from below, from the triangular earth. With both, human beings copy the universe—they have more or less rounded heads above, and the earth-forces form them from below.

Look for it sometime. You will find in most varied ways man's tendency (and that of animals) to triangular formation in the jaws; this comes from the earth. Forces work upwards from the earth and imprint the triangle into him. And the universe works downwards from above and moulds the rounded form. It is very interesting!

That is knowledge that may be gained if one really penetrates genuine science. If one is free from thought, then one talks all sorts of nonsense. And in our time all sorts of nonsense is talked that cannot lead to an understanding of the reality of things.

So, gentlemen, let us speak further about this next Saturday.

What is the aim of anthroposophy? Biela's comet

Rudolf Steiner: Good morning, gentlemen! Has an interesting question occurred to anyone?

Question: What is anthroposophy actually? What is its aim and its task in the world?

Rudolf Steiner: The questioner wants to know what anthroposophy is and what its significance is for humanity in general. I would also add, its significance for the working class.

It is obviously difficult to speak briefly about these matters. Those who have been here for a considerable time will have become more and more convinced that something like anthroposophy had to enter the evolution of humanity. Those who have not been here long will naturally have some difficulty and only gradually be able to understand.

First and foremost, we must realize that people are little inclined to accept something new when it comes into the world. Remarkable examples could be given of how new scientific discoveries have been received. Think, for instance, of the extent to which everything today has been affected by the discovery of the power of steam and the invention of the steam engine. Think what the world would be like today if there were no steam engines in their many different forms! When the steam engine was first invented, a small boat, driven by steam, made its way up a river and was smashed up by the peasants because they said they were not going to put up with such a thing; it was unsuitable for human beings! Nor has it always been the peasants who behaved in that way. When an account of meteorites was given for the first time in a learned assembly in Paris, the lecturer was declared to be a fool. And I told you recently about Julius Robert Mayer, who is regarded today as a most illustrious man and a very great scholar—he was shut up in an asylum!

What happened with the railroads was particularly remarkable. As you know, they have not been in existence very long; they came into use for the first time in the nineteenth century. Before that, people had to travel by stagecoach. When it was proposed to build the first railroad between Berlin and Potsdam, the Director of Mail-coaches[34] said that two went empty from Berlin to Potsdam every week, so he couldn't imagine what use railroads would be. It didn't occur to him that once the railroads were there, more people would travel by them than by the stagecoach.

Even more interesting was the attitude of a body of medical men,[35] in the forties of the nineteenth century. When the railroad from Fürth to Nuremberg was being built, these learned gentlemen declared that the work should be stopped, because the speed could very easily make a traveller ill by damaging his nerves. When people refused to accept this ban, they were told that high plank walls must be erected on both sides of the tracks, in order to protect the peasants from concussion when trains passed! You can still read about this in delightful old documents. But despite all this opposition, the railroads made rapid headway. And anthroposophy, too, will make its way in the world, simply because it is a necessity, because nothing in the world can really be understood unless the spiritual foundation of things is recognized and known.

It is not anthroposophy's aim to oppose science; it has actually arisen because of natural science. But science with its elaborate instruments and remarkably clever experiments has discovered a mass of facts which—in the way it presents them—cannot really be understood. Nor will they ever be understood until it is realized that the spiritual world is behind everything and within everything.

Let us take a very ordinary, practical matter: the eating of potatoes. Once upon a time there were no potatoes in Europe; they were introduced into Europe from foreign countries. It is claimed that Sir Francis Drake[36] introduced potatoes, but that is not correct; they came from a different source. Yet in Offenburg there is a memorial statue of Drake. During the war we were once obliged to stop at Offenburg, and I was curious to find out why this statue had been erected. I looked in the encyclopaedia and there it was: a memorial statue of Drake stands in Offenburg because he was the man who first brought potatoes to Europe.

But now what about potatoes? Suppose a scientist or a doctor were asked to say what effect potatoes have when they are eaten. As you know, potatoes have become a staple. In some places it is very difficult to dissuade people from feeding almost exclusively on them. What does the modern scientist do when he tests potatoes for their nutritional value? He makes a laboratory investigation to find what substances are contained in the potato. He finds carbohydrates, which consist of carbon, oxygen and hydrogen in definite proportions; he also discovers that in the human body these substances are finally transformed into a kind of sugar. But he gets no further than that; nor can he do so. For think of this. If some animal is fed on milk, it may thrive. But if the milk is analysed for its chemical components and if these chemical components are given to the animal instead of the milk, it will waste away for lack of nourishment. Why is that? It is because something is working in the milk in addition to chemical components. And in the potato, too, there is something more than the mere chemical components; there is the spiritual element. A spiritual element works everywhere, in all of nature.

If in spiritual science (anthroposophy is, after all, only a name) genuine investigation is made into how the potato nourishes the human being, the potato is found to be something that is not completely digested by the digestive organs, but it passes into the head through the lymph glands, through the blood, in such a way that the head itself must also serve as a digestive organ for the potato. When potatoes are eaten in large quantities, the head becomes a kind of stomach and also digests.

There is a very great difference between eating potatoes and, for instance, good, wholesome bread. When wholesome bread is eaten, the material part of the rye or wheat is digested properly and healthily in the digestive tract. And consequently only what is spiritual in the rye or wheat comes into the head, where it belongs.

This kind of knowledge can never be derived from natural science. When things are genuinely investigated with respect to their spiritual quality, it becomes apparent that in this modern age humanity has been seriously injured by an excessive consumption of potatoes. Spiritual science finds that the eating of potatoes has played a very large part in the general deterioration of health in recent centuries. That is a crude example of how spiritual science can investigate the excellent results of natural science by taking them as the basis for its research.

But there is something else as well. Every substance in the world can be examined to determine its spiritual quality. That is the only way in which real remedies for illnesses can be discovered. So spiritual science provides a very definite foundation for medicine as well.

Spiritual science is only an extension of natural science; it is by no means something that refutes natural science. And besides that, we have in spiritual science something that investigates the spiritual in a scientific way and therefore does not ask people simply to believe things that are said.

Matters of faith are thus replaced by scientific inquiry. It must also be said that in all fields science acquires a certain amount of knowledge. Humanity does not, of course, have to concern itself with every scientific detail, but every individual ought at least to have some basic knowledge and understanding of the world.

I'd like to tell you something that will show you how important it is to be able to recognize how the spirit actually works. In the year 1773, a rumour suddenly spread in Paris that a distinguished scholar[37] was to give a lecture in a certain learned Society, in which he would prove that a comet was about to collide with the earth and destroy it. In those days it was believed that such a thing could be proven exactly and scientifically. So at that time, in the eighteenth century, when superstition was still rife, a terrible panic spread through the whole of Paris. If we read the records of what happened in Paris at that time, we find that there were enormous numbers of miscarriages; the women gave birth prematurely out of sheer terror. People who were seriously ill, died; others became ill from fright. There was terrific agitation throughout Paris because it became known that a learned man would announce the forthcoming collision of a comet with the earth and the consequent destruction of the earth. The police, who as you know are ever on the alert, forbade the lecture, so the people never discovered what the professor had intended to say. But there was anxiety nevertheless! You may now ask whether the professor who wanted to give the lecture was right or wrong.

Well, the matter is not quite so simple as that. For since Copernicus propounded his new theory of the universe, everything has become a matter of calculation, and the calculations at that time led to the following conclusion. The sun is taken to be the centre of the universe; then come Mercury, Venus, Moon, earth and Mars, then the asteroids, then Jupiter, then Saturn. And there are also the comets and their orbits. The earth is circling and people can calculate when it will reach a certain point where the comet collides with it. Bang! — according to the calculations — they will collide. And at that time, gentlemen, they would actually have collided — only the comet was so small that it dissolved in the air! Not exactly in the air over Paris, but somewhere else. The calculation was therefore quite correct, but there was no ground for anxiety.

In the year 1832 there was an even stranger story. For then it was calculated that a comet — it was Biela's comet — was about to cross the earth's orbit and would pass quite near to the earth. This comet was not such a midget as the other, and was likely to be more dangerous. But the calculation turned out happily, for it showed that when the comet passed the earth it would still be 13,000,000 miles away — and that's at least a tiny distance away, don't you think? So there was no need to fear that the earth would be destroyed. But even so, people were very alarmed at the time, because heavenly bodies are mutually attracted to each other, and it had to be expected that the comet would cause great convulsions in the oceans and seas through the force of gravity, and so on. Nothing very special happened — there was, it is true, a general unrest in nature, but nothing of particular interest. The comet was 13,000,000 miles away — the sun is 13 times farther away — so no harm was done to the earth at that time.

In 1872, when I was a boy living with my parents at a small railway station, we were always reading in the papers: 'The world will be destroyed!' — for the comet was due to appear again. Certain comets always do return, and this one, on its return, would now be nearer to the earth and therefore more dangerous. This remarkable comet had already come in 1845/46 and again in 1852 — but it had then split in two! Each half had become thinner in consequence of the split. And what was there to be seen in 1872?

Something like a gleaming rain of shooting stars, a great number of shooting stars! The comet had indeed come nearer but it had split and was casting off finer matter that came down like shining rain. Everyone could see it, for when such a tremendous array of shooting stars occurs in the night, they can be seen coming down from the sky. And some people who saw this happening believed that the Day of Judgment had come. Again there was great alarm. However, the shooting stars dissolved in the atmosphere.

Now think of this: if the comet had remained whole, our earth would have suffered badly in the year 1872. As I said, papers reached our railway station announcing the imminent destruction of the earth. The astronomers had calculated the precise time. According to scientific reckoning this was quite correct. And it is probably better to pass over in silence the fact that many people at that time paid large fees to their priests – to be safely absolved from their sins. In 1773 too, in Paris, the father-confessors had made a great deal of money because people wanted to be absolved from their sins immediately!

There was an astronomer called Littrov[38] who made a noteworthy calculation about what would have happened if things had remained as they were in the year 1832, that is, if the comet had not split up as it subsequently did. In the nineteenth century it was still 13 million miles away from the earth, but every time it came, it came closer. Littrov reckoned quite correctly that in September 1872 there would be a danger of the comet colliding with the earth. If the comet had then reached the point which as a matter of fact it did not actually reach in that year until 27 November, it would not just have been a matter of meteor showers but it would have been a serious matter. Such things do indeed happen. Littrov calculated that in 1933 (it is now 1924, so in nine years' time), if the comet had remained as it still was in the eighteenth century, a collision would be inevitable and the earth would be demolished. The calculation was correct to the breadth of a hair. But the comet had not remained as it was! And so people could say: 'The comet has been merciful, for if it were still fiery, in 1933 it would strike the earth in such a way that all the seas would surge from the Equator to the North Pole and the whole earth would perish.' Yes, the comet split up and it cast off the substance that had become too heavy for it, in the form of harmless meteorites.

So you see, if that comet had not been merciful, none of us would be sitting here today! That is a fact. What has finally happened is this. The comet no longer appears as a comet, but on those dates when in the ordinary course of events it would have appeared, there are always meteor showers. Gradually through the centuries it is casting off its entire substance. Soon it will no longer be visible because it will have given up its substance to the universe and to the earth.

But now I want to show you another angle on this matter. It is obvious that in the course of human evolution man's spiritual faculties are constantly changing. Those who do not believe this simply do not understand the spiritual evolution of mankind. For think of it, all our modern discoveries would have been made long ago if people had possessed the same faculties of mind that they possess today. In ancient times their mental and spiritual faculties were not less, but they were different. I have explained this to you in the most varied ways, also in answer to questions on the subject.

And now to return to the comets. The comet of which I've been speaking is not the only one that was merciful enough to split up and dissolve in cosmic space at the right time. A large number of other comets have done the same. A great deal of superstition has always been connected with the subject of comets. Anthroposophy approaches the matter in an absolutely scientific way.

But now, what will happen if we go on developing in the same way as we are developing today? Mankind is now so dreadfully clever! Just compare a person of today with all his cleverness, with all that he has learnt in school, with someone living in the twelfth or thirteenth century, when very, very few people could write. Think of this. There is a beautiful poem by Wolfram von Eschenbach,[39] who was a nobleman of the thirteenth century. He composed the poem, but he could not write, so he was obliged to call in a priest to whom he dictated it. And that poem was the *Parsival* on which Wagner based his opera. So you see, in those days people had different faculties. We need go no further back than the twelfth or thirteenth century. At that time a nobleman could not write. Wolfram von Eschenbach could read but not write.

These faculties of ours do not come to us ready-made; they are developed. And if things continue as they are at present, when between the ages of 7 and 14 we are crammed with scientific knowledge of every kind—there is, of course, a good side to this as well—we'll gradually all suffer from something that was previously quite unknown and that is now so prevalent. We'll all suffer from what you call 'nerves', from nervous illnesses. This shows you that those wise doctors in the forties of the last century who believed so 'stupidly' that people would not be able to live if railways were built, were—given the knowledge they had—not so stupid after all! For everything they knew at that time convinced them that if a person travels in trains, he will eventually become utterly incapable of work, lose his memory, exhaust his nerves and become shaky and abnormally restless. The science of their day justified them in their conviction. Moreover, what they said was correct, absolutely correct.

But there is one thing they left out of account. People have indeed become more nervous. You yourselves, when you get home from work, are not quite like the people of the thirties and forties of the last century who would simply put on their nightcaps in the evening and be snug and cosy without any trace of 'nerves'. The world has certainly changed in this respect. But what was it that those Nuremberg doctors could not know at that time? They could not know that while they were learning all these things from their science, the comet was already in the process of dissolving. And what has the comet done? It gives us meteors, fine meteorite rain. Instead of colliding with the earth and breaking people's heads it is giving all its substance away, and this substance, every part of it, is in the earth. Every few years the comet gives something to the earth. And people who want to live by science alone and who will not admit that the earth receives something from the cosmos are every bit as stupid as someone who would say that when a person eats a piece of bread it is not in him. Obviously, what the comet gives us is in the earth, but science takes no notice of it. Where, then, is it to be found? It goes into the air, is passed from the air into the water, from the water into the roots of the plants, from the roots of the plant into the food on our tables. From there it passes into our bodies. We eat what the comet has been giving us for centuries! This, however, has long been spiritualized. Instead of the comet putting an end to the earth in 1933, its substance has long been in the earth as a means of earthly nourishment, and it is a remedy, a cosmic remedy: it alleviates nervous troubles in human beings.

There, you see, you have a little piece of history. The comets appear out there in the heavens, and after a time they find their way into us out of the earth. By that time their substance has become spiritualized.

Such things play a real part in human life. History can no longer be presented in a philistine, literal way; account must now be taken of what is going on in the world spiritually. That is possible only when light is shed upon the world through anthroposophy. You may say: 'Oh well, life will go on just the same. All that comet business shows that it doesn't matter if we're stupid, and there is no need for us to bother about it!' Although people want to be enlightened, in practice they are dreadfully fatalistic, thinking that everything in the world will go on 'as it is meant to'. Well, perhaps—but there is also the opportunity either to adopt a true science or to ignore it.

You know, gentlemen, that for years I gave lectures to workers.[40] And I often called attention to a splendid lecture given by Lassalle[41] in 1863 entitled 'Science and the Worker'. I don't know whether there is still any widespread knowledge of it, but in the meantime I've grown older and I've witnessed the rise of the labour movement. From my parents' house in the early seventies of the nineteenth century I could look out of the window and watch the first Social Democrats—they still wore big hats, 'democrats' hats'—marching out into the woods where they held their meetings. So I've seen all stages in the development of the movement. At that time Lassalle was still greatly venerated; wherever workers' meetings took place, busts of him were displayed. Today these things have been more or less forgotten, for 50 years have elapsed since then. I was ten or eleven years old at the time, but I had started to pay attention to what was happening. Lassalle had given this lecture, 'Science and the Worker', about eight or nine years earlier. In it he had stressed that science is absolutely crucial for the solution of the whole labour problem and that through science the workers have developed a social outlook that has occurred to no one else. In a certain sense this was an extremely important thing that he said.

But now think what has happened since that time. I ask you: are you satisfied? Can you be satisfied with the way the labour problem has developed, with the form it has taken? Are there not many widespread complaints about the way the workers are tyrannized by their labour unions and so forth? These things are in the air and the worker is aware of them. But what he does not perceive is where these conditions come from. Where do they come from? The answer is that the solution to the labour problem cannot actually be found without science. Formerly, these problems were solved through religion and the like; today they must be dealt with by means of science. But this requires genuinely scientific thinking, which was nowhere to be found because attention was invariably riveted upon matter, and science itself was sheer materialism. None of our social problems will ever be solved until science becomes spiritual again.

This can happen only when science is prepared to look for the spiritual element in every single thing, whether it be a potato or a comet. For spiritual knowledge alone enables us to investigate the true connections between things. The true context of social problems, too, can only be discovered through spiritual knowledge. These connections must be fully understood; and when they are, it will be found that the things to which Marxism has given prominence, for example, were extremely well meant, but they were based upon an erroneous science. I will show you why this was the case. Nothing that is based on an erroneous science can really prosper.

Marx's arguments and calculations are uncommonly astute, uncommonly clever, and cannot be denied, because the principles upon which he bases them are from a science that is purely materialistic. Everything tallies, just as it tallied for the astronomers who calculated that the comet would collide with the earth in 1773, but in fact the comet had dissolved to such an extent that no harm was done to the earth! The conclusions reached by Marx are based upon an equally meticulous but equally incomplete science.

One of his calculations was the following. He said: 'When someone is working, he uses up inner forces. The forces are given up to his work and in the evening he is fatigued. During the day he has used up a definite quantity of force or energy. Naturally, the worker needs something that enables his forces to be restored. It can be precisely calculated how much pay will make it possible for the worker to restore his forces.' Yes, but along these lines expounded by Marx, does one really arrive at the right and proper wage for labour? Does one arrive at it in that way? Obviously, up to now no great progress has been made in this direction. But the fact is that it simply cannot be arrived at in that way, because although the science itself is admirable it is untrue.

Think of someone who does no work the whole day long, someone who has private wealth. He can go for walks, or he can move from one armchair to another — and from morning till night he's using up his forces just the same. I've noticed at workers' concerts that those who had been working all day were much less fatigued than the well-to-do people who had done nothing at all. The latter kept yawning, while the others were bright and lively.

You see, there is an error in the calculation. The forces used up inwardly in our organism are not the ones we use in our outer work or labour. That is why the calculation cannot be based on scientific foundations. The whole matter must be approached in a different way; it must be based upon the intrinsic dignity of man, upon his rights as a human being, and so forth. The same applies in many other spheres. And the consequence is that science, as it has developed up to the present day, is responsible for dreadful confusion of thought, for ignorance in the social sphere.

Spiritual science will show you what nutritive value there is in potatoes, in cabbage, in salt, and so on. And then you can work out what the human being needs in order to be healthy and to thrive. You can only get at this through spiritual science, only on the basis of knowledge that comes from spiritual science. Then you can proceed to the study of social problems. And then the labour problem will look quite different. It will finally be given a sounder basis, because everything relating to it will be looked at from a spiritual point of view.

People today simply don't understand how things are connected in this world; they believe everything goes on just as it is. But that is not true. People must understand how things in the world are constantly changing. And the greatest misfortune, one might say, is that in earlier times humanity was superstitious and now it is scientific! For little by little, superstition has crept into science itself. Today we have a natural science that is full of superstitions. People believe that when their stomach is full of potatoes they have had a nourishing meal. The truth is that the health of their head is impaired, because the head itself then has to become a digestive organ.

Thus all problems should be dealt with in such a way that the spiritual aspect is not ignored as it has been for a long time now. It should be included in every consideration. In the sixties and seventies of the last century, people said: 'The worker must have science!' — and rightly so. But it must be a *true* science. In those days it was not in existence. Now it is to be found in spiritual science, which has the name anthroposophy. Anthroposophy refuses to put the cart before the horse as was done formerly. It will put spirit before matter, where it belongs. Then people will discover how things really are. And they will find proper educational methods. There will be a pedagogy that educates children as they really should be educated. Upon that, very much, very much indeed depends. And then human beings will find their right place in society.

In a single hour, naturally, I can give no more than hints; but we have arranged these lectures so that you could raise questions that you want me to talk about. And so perhaps I should speak further on today's subject in the next session. Today I could only lay the foundation. But at least you have been able to glean something about the real aim of spiritual science.

So we'll meet again next Wednesday.

Where do we come from? — earth life and star wisdom

Rudolf Steiner: Good morning, gentlemen! I would like to add a few words to what we were considering last time, and then perhaps someone will have a new question.

The question that was asked concerning man's origin can be rightly understood and answered only by looking back at the whole evolution of humanity. The assertion that human beings were originally animal-like, that they had an animal-like intelligence, and so forth, is nothing but a science fairy-tale. It is contradicted by what can be discovered about earliest historical times, and what — even though poetic in form — indicates the existence of great wisdom among the human beings who lived during those primeval epochs on earth. At that time people did not feel inequality among themselves as they feel it today. The feeling of inequality always comes to the fore in an epoch when people have more or less lost real knowledge.

Only think how at a certain period in ancient Egypt slavery was widespread. But slavery did not always exist; it developed at a time when people had lost real knowledge of the world, had lost real science, and no longer knew what slavery signified. And if you think intelligently you will certainly ask yourselves: Why is it that, for instance, such an energetic labour movement had to arise?

Naturally it was bound to arise because conditions made it necessary, because people had come to feel that things could not go on as they were, and they wanted to call attention to how conditions should be bettered. What makes the labour problem such a burning question is the fact that industry and all the various discoveries and inventions have gone in one particular direction. Before the spread of industry there was not such misery and hardship. Why is it, then, that the advent of industry has brought this burden in its train?

As every reasonable person will admit, those less numerous human beings who do not live in actual need – the capitalists, as they are usually called – do not create this need deliberately for the pure joy of it. Naturally, they would prefer the needs of all human beings to be satisfied. Obviously, that must be taken into account. But then this other question arises: Why is it that the few who reach leading positions lack the capacity to change conditions so that the needs of the masses can be satisfied?

It is always the few leaders in the trade unions upon whom all the others depend. As things have developed, it is quite natural that it is always the few who lead, but they lack clear insight. And the masses of workers feel that these few do not themselves know what should be done. It has become obvious, especially just recently, that these few do not know what they should be doing. So one must say that something is obviously lacking. And from the view of spiritual science, the thing lacking is knowledge of the spiritual world. This knowledge would confirm that it is absolutely untrue to say that at the beginning of their evolution human beings were unintelligent, dull, and that now they are enlightened. That is the general opinion today and it is simply not true.

At the beginning of their existence on the earth, human beings possessed a knowledge not only of what was on the earth but also of the stars in the heavens. The reason why this knowledge has nowadays degenerated into super-stition – I have often spoken of this – is that, as time went on, these things were no longer investigated and hence came to be misunderstood. Originally there was a widespread knowledge of the stars; today the only knowledge of the stars that exists is one that makes calculations about them. But it is unable to penetrate to their spiritual reality. If a being living on Mars were to know only as much about the earth as our ordinary consciousness, our ordinary science, knows about Mars, that Mars being would believe that there is not a single soul on the earth—whereas actually there are 15 to 20 hundred million souls on the earth! It is the same with the ideas people hold now about the stars; actually the stars are full of souls—only the souls are different.

Of course you may say one can't see into the world of stars, so one can't know or observe the conditions there. That is an enormous error! Why can a person standing here see the piano over there? Because his eyes are such that he is able to see it. His eyes are not over there in the piano. In exactly the same way—as spiritual science, or anthroposophy, shows—if a human being not only develops from childhood to the level to which our modern education takes him, but develops further than that, he will in very truth be able to perceive what is spiritual in the stars, just as humanity originally perceived it. And then he will know that the stars have an influence upon the human being, each star a different influence. If, for example, it can be shown that Mars has an influence upon the development of grubs into cockchafers it can also be shown that all the stars have an influence upon man's spiritual life. They do indeed! But this knowledge of the stars has entirely disappeared—and what has replaced it?

In former times, when people looked at the moon, they knew that from the moon come the forces for all reproduction on the earth. No being would have offspring if the moon did not send to earth the forces of propagation. No being or creature would grow if the forces of growth did not come from the sun. No human being would be able to think if the forces of thinking did not come from Saturn. But all that people know today is the speed at which Saturn moves, the speed at which the moon moves, and whether there are a few extinct volcanoes on the moon. They know nothing more and don't want to know anything more. They simply find out by calculation what they want to know about the stars.

But now let us turn from the world of stars to the world of human beings. Industry has arrived on the scene. In the age when all that people could do about the stars was to make calculations, they began to do the same in the domain of industry. They did nothing but reckon and calculate, with the result that they forgot man altogether. They treated the human being himself as if he were part of a machine. And so the conditions have come about that prevail today. Conditions will never be satisfactory if people merely calculate what kind of conditions ought to prevail on the earth; they will have to know something beside that. That is the point. But then it must be admitted that human knowledge has deteriorated to a terrible extent in the very age that claims to be 'enlightened'.

I told you that at a recent Farmers' Conference it was unanimously agreed that all agricultural products have been deteriorating for decades. The reason for this deterioration is that, with the exception of certain peasants who have instinctively hung on to some of the knowledge people used to have, nothing is really known about the way to take care of a farm. But how is such knowledge acquired? Certainly it can never be acquired by calculation, for instance by knowing that the moon will be full again in 28 days, but only by knowing how moon forces work in the propagation of grain, and so forth. This knowledge has been entirely forgotten. People don't even know what goes on in the soil in their fields.

And they know still less what is going on in the human world.

Social science has produced nothing more than one series after another of calculations. Capital, working hours, wages, are nothing but figures that have been calculated. And calculating does not get to grips with human life, or indeed with any life at all. The curse of the modern age is that everything is to be merely calculated. Instead of things being merely calculated, they should be studied and observed as they actually are, and this is only possible through first gaining knowledge of the stars. Today, the moment people hear the phrase 'knowledge of the stars', they say immediately: 'That's idiotic! We've known for a long time that the stars have no influence whatever.' But to assert that the stars have no influence upon what is happening on the earth, that, gentlemen, is the real idiocy! And the consequence is that there is no real knowledge left. That is a concrete fact. Take capital, for instance. It can be expressed in figures, it can be counted — and what is the result? If capital is merely a matter of calculation, it is of no importance who owns the capital, whether a single individual or everyone in common. For the same results will invariably ensue. Not until we take hold of life again so that our concern centres upon the human being as the prime reality, not until then will there be a social science capable of doing anything effective, a social science capable of really achieving something.

That is why I also like to say this: Let us see what will come about through anthroposophy. It is, of course, still only in its infancy, and naturally it appears to be similar in many respects to other science. But it will develop gradually into a complete knowledge of the human being. In the domain of education, for instance, it has already given rise to the Waldorf School. Not until this stage of knowledge has been reached will it be possible to apply anthroposophical science effectively to social problems. Today you can only realize that the world's current knowledge is incapable of really effective intervention in life; it stops short everywhere.

That is what I wanted to add. Are you satisfied so far? (Yes, yes!) Of course, a great deal could still be said, but there will be other opportunities for considering many aspects of the subject.

So now, has anyone else thought of a question?

Question: Can anything be known about man's origin? Where he comes from?

Rudolf Steiner: That is a question about which many of you who have been here for some time have heard a great deal from me. Those of you who have come recently are naturally interested in such questions, so those who have already heard my answers will perhaps be willing to hear them again.

When we look at the human being as he walks about on the earth nowadays, we see his body first and foremost. We also notice that he thinks and feels. If we look at a chair, no matter how long we wait, it doesn't begin to move about— because it cannot exercise will. We perceive that the human being wills. But speaking generally it can be said that we really see only the body.

And it is very easy to form the opinion that this body constitutes the whole of man. Moreover, if this is believed, many arguments can be found to prove it. (You see, in anthroposophy other people's opinions cannot be treated lightly. All points of view must be seriously considered.) And so it can be pointed out, for instance, that people can lose their memory if they take poison and are not immediately killed by it. The implication is that the body is a machine and everything depends upon the running of the machine. If the blood vessels burst in a person's brain and the blood presses on the nerves, such a man may lose not only his memory but his whole intelligence. So it can be said that everything is dependent upon the body. But that kind of thinking does not hold water if one really examines it thoroughly. It simply does not hold water. If it did, we could say that man thinks with his brain. But what is actually going on in the brain when a person thinks?

Well, a real investigation of the human body shows that it is absolutely incorrect to say that when a person is thinking, something constructive is going on in his brain. On the contrary, something is always being destroyed, demolished, when he is thinking. Substances in the brain are being broken down, destroyed. Death on a small scale is perpetually taking place there.

The final death that happens once and for all means that the whole body is destroyed; but what happens all at once in the entire body when a person dies is also taking place throughout the body during life, in a piecemeal process. Man excretes not only through his organs of excretion, the urine, faeces, sweat, but in other ways as well. Just think what your head would look like if you never had your hair cut! Something is excreted there, too. And think of the claws you'd have if you never cut your nails! But not only that. We are continually sloughing off our skin – we just don't notice it. We are casting off substance all the time. In the case of the urine and faeces the process is not very significant, because for the most part these simply contain what has been eaten, material that has not gone into the whole body, whereas what is excreted in the nails has passed through the whole body.

Suppose you take your scissors and cut a fingernail. What you now cut away you took in, you ate, seven or eight years ago. What you ate went into the blood and nerves and passed through the whole body. It needed seven or eight years to do that. Now you cut it away. Just think of the body you have today, the body in which you are sitting there. If you had sat there seven or eight years ago, it would have been in quite another body! The body you had then has been cast away, has been sweated away, has been cut away with the nails, cut away with the hair. The entire body as it once was, has gone—with the exception of the bones and the like—and within a period of seven or eight years has been entirely renewed.

So now we must ask ourselves: Does thinking originate from the constant upbuilding of the body or from the constant breaking-down of the body? That is an important question. If you have something in your body that brings about too much synthesis or upbuilding—shall I say, if you drink one tiny glass too much, or not just one (most people can manage that), but if you drink until you know you've had more than is good for you—what happens then, gentlemen? The blood becomes very active and a terribly rapid process of upbuilding takes place. When that happens, when the blood becomes too tumultuous, a person loses consciousness. Thinking is not the result of an upbuilding process in the brain, but of a process of small, piecemeal destruction. If no breaking-down process took place in the human body, the human being would simply not be able to think.

So the fact is that thinking does not arise when we build up the body but from our continual killing of it bit by bit. That is why we have to sleep, because we don't do any thinking then. What is continually being demolished through our thinking is quickly restored in sleep. So waking and sleeping show us that while we are thinking, death is always taking place in the body on a small scale.

But now picture for a moment not a person's body, but his clothing. If you take off all your clothes you are not, it is true, fit for the drawing-room, but you are still there, and you can put on different clothes. That is what we do through the whole of our earthly life. Every seven or eight years we put on a new body and discard the other. With animals there is a clear illustration of this. If you were to collect all the skins that a snake sloughs off every year, you would find that after a certain number of years it has discarded not only the skin but the whole of its body. In our case, of course, this is not so noticeable! And what about the birds? They moult. What are they doing when they moult? They're discarding part of their body; and after a period of a few years they've discarded it all, with the exception of the bones. What is it that remains?

You yourself are sitting there today although you have nothing at all of the body you had some eight years ago. And yet there you are, sitting here. You created a new body for yourself. The soul, gentlemen, sits there. The spirit and soul sit there. The spirit and soul work on the body, building it up all the time. If you go for a walk and find a large pile of stones somewhere, you know that a house is going to be built; you will certainly not assume that the stones will suddenly have feet and will place themselves very neatly one above the other and build themselves into a house! Well, just as little do substances assemble to form themselves into our body.

We receive our first body from our father and mother; but this body is cast off entirely, and after seven or eight years we have a new one. We do not get this one from our parents; we ourselves have to build it up. Where does it come from? The body we had during the first years of life came from our parents; we could not have had a body without them. But what builds up the second body comes from the spiritual world. I do not mean the substance, but the active principle, the essential being, that is what comes out of the spiritual world. So we can say that when the human being is born, the body he has for the first seven or eight years of his life comes from his father and mother, but the soul and spiritual entity come from the spiritual world. And every seven or eight years the human being exchanges his body but retains all of himself that is spiritual. After a certain time the body is worn out and what once entered it as spirit and soul goes back again into the spiritual world. Man comes from the spiritual world and returns to the spiritual world.

You can see, this is also something that has been entirely forgotten—simply because today people have become thoughtless and do not penetrate to the reality of things. Once they have seen how the body is renewed over and over again, they will realize that the force which brings about the renewal is a soul force working within the body.

And now, gentlemen, what do you eat? Let us consider the different foodstuffs a human being eats. The simplest substance of all is protein. Not only in eggs but in the greatest variety of foodstuffs, in plants too, there is protein. Then we eat fat; we eat what are called carbohydrates—in potatoes, for instance—and minerals. All other substances are composite substances; we eat them, take them into ourselves. They come from the earth; they are entirely dependent upon the earth. Everything we take in through the mouth is entirely dependent upon the earth. But now we don't take things in only through the mouth; we also breathe, and through our breathing we take in substances from the air. Usually this process is described very simply by saying the human being breathes in oxygen and breathes out carbon dioxide—as if he did nothing but breathe in, breathe out, breathe in, breathe out! But that is not the whole story. Very fine, rarefied substances are contained in the air we breathe. And we live not only on what we eat but also on these nourishing substances from the air. If we did nothing but eat, we would be obliged to replace our body very often, for what we eat is very rapidly transformed in the body. Only think how troublesome it is for someone when he does not get rid of what ought to be excreted within about 24 hours. The food that is eaten and then excreted passes through a rapid process. If we lived only on what we eat, we certainly wouldn't need seven or eight years to replace our body. It is because we take in very delicate, rarefied nourishment through the air, which is a slow process, that the replacement takes seven or eight years.

It is very important to know that we take in nourishment from the air. The food we eat is used, for example, for the constant renewing of our head. But the nourishment we need in order, shall we say, to have fingernails does not come from what we eat but from the substances we draw from the air. And so we are nourished through eating and through breathing.

But now the really important fact is that when we take in nourishment from the cosmos through our breathing we take in not only substance but also, at the same time, the element of soul. The substance is in such a fine, rarefied state that the soul is able to live in it everywhere. So we may say that man takes in bodily substance through his food; through his breathing he takes in, he lives within a soul element. But it is not the case that with every inhalation we take a piece of soul into ourselves and then with every exhalation breathe out a piece of soul again. In that event we would always be discarding the soul. No—it is like this. With our very first breath we take the soul into ourselves, and it is then the soul that brings about the breathing in us. And with our very last breath we set the soul free so that it can go back to the spiritual world.

And now that we know these things, we can make some calculations. Most of you will already know what follows, but it may still surprise you. If you investigate, you will find that a human being draws 18 breaths a minute. Now reckon how many breaths he draws in a day: 18 breaths a minute, $18 \times 60 = 1080$ breaths an hour; in 24 hours, $24 \times 1080 = 25,920$ breaths a day.

And now let us calculate — we can do so approximately — how many days a human being lives on the earth. For the sake of simplicity let us take 72 years as the average length of human life, and 360 days in a year; 72 years × 360 days = 25,920 days in a man's life. And that is the number of breaths a man draws in a day! So we can say, the human being lives as many days in his life as he draws breaths in one day.

Now we know there are flies which only live one day — and there could also conceivably be $\frac{1}{18}$-of-a-minute creatures! (For the length of time is not the essential point.) So if the human being were to die every time he breathes we could say he breathes the soul in and out again with every breath. Yet he remains — remains alive for 25,920 days.

So now let us reckon those 72 years as a single breath. As I said before, with his first breath the human being breathes his soul in and with his last breath he breathes it out again. Assuming now that he lives an average of 72 years, we can say that this inbreathing and outbreathing of the soul lasts for a period of 72 years. Taking this period to be one cosmic day, we would again have to multiply 72 × 360 to get a cosmic year: 25,920! If we take the life of a human being as one cosmic day, we get the cosmic year: 25,920 cosmic days!

But this number has still another meaning. On the 21st of March, the day of the beginning of spring, the sun rises at the present time in the constellation of Pisces. But it rises only once at that exact point. The point at which it rises shifts all the time. About five hundred years ago it did not rise in Pisces (the Fishes) but in Aries (the Ram), and earlier still in Taurus (the Bull). So the sun passes through the whole zodiac, finally getting back to Pisces. At a definite time it will rise again at exactly the same point, having made a complete circuit. How long does the sun need for this? It needs 25,920 years to go around and return to the same rising point at the beginning of spring.

When we have breathed 25,920 times, we have completed one day. Our soul remains while the breaths alternate. When we have completed 25,920 days, we have awakened as often as we have slept. In sleep, as we know, we do not think, we do not move, we are inactive. During sleep our spirit and soul have gone off to the spiritual world for a few hours; at waking we get them back again. Just as we let the breath go out and come back 18 times a minute, so in a day we let the soul leave once and return. Sleeping and waking, you see, are simply more lengthy breaths. We do a shorter breathing 18 times a minute. Our longer breathing is sleeping and waking. And the longest breathing is our breathing in the soul and spirit when we are born and breathing it out again when we die. But there is still the very longest breathing of all; for we accompany the sun as it completes its circuit of 25,920 years; we go into the world of the stars. When we enter the soul realm, gentlemen, at that very moment we leave the earth and go to the world of the stars.

So — these are just the first foundations for an answer to the question which the gentleman asked. Just think what order and regularity prevail in the universe if again and again we get the number 25,920! Man's breathing is a living expression of the course of the sun. That is a fact of tremendous significance.

So — I have begun to answer the question. I will continue next Saturday at 9 o'clock.[42]

Notes

1 'The little Plateau experiment', worked out by the physicist J.A.F. Plateau, 1801–83. Compare the description by Vincent Knauer in his lectures, 'The Main Problem of Philosophy', Vienna and Leipzig 1892: 'One of the nicest experiments is the Plateau experiment. A mixture of water and alcohol is prepared, having the exact weight of pure olive oil. Into this is poured a rather large drop of oil. This does not float on top of the liquid but sinks to the middle of it, in the form of a ball. A small disc of cardboard is then perforated in the centre by a long needle and lowered carefully into the middle of the ball of oil, so that the edge of the cardboard becomes the "equator" of the ball. The disc is now set into motion, at first slowly, then faster and faster. Naturally the movement is imparted to the ball of oil, and as a result of the strength of the movement, parts of the oil drop away and continue the movement separately for some time, first in circles, then revolving as tiny balls. In this way there arises something surprisingly similar to our planetary system: in the centre the largest globe, like our sun, and moving around it smaller balls and rings, like our planets with their moons.'

2 This lecture was postponed to Thursday, 3 July.

3 This lecture was postponed to Monday, 7 July.

4 Paris, 25 May–16 June 1906: *L'Esotérisme chrétien/Esquisse d'une cosmogonie psychologique*, Paris 1957. English edition: *An Esoteric Cosmology*, St. George Publications, New York, 1978.

5 Eugen Dubois, 1858–1940, Dutch military doctor and geologist. Discovered remains of Java man, a creature intermediate between ape and man. See his publication *Pithecanthropus erectus, eine menschenähnliche Übergangsform auf Java*, Batavia, 1894.

6 The Second International Congress, Vienna, 1–12 June 1922. See *The Tension between East and West*, Anthroposophic Press, New York, 1983.

7   Berthold Schwarz, Franciscan monk, Freiburg, around 1300.

8   Johann Gutenberg, 1394–1468.

9   Laotse, Chinese philosopher, sixth century BC.

10   Confucius, 531–478 BC, Chinese teacher of ethics and philosopher.

11   The philosopher Karl Ludwig Michelet, 1801–93, and the theologian and philosopher Eduard Zeller, 1814–1908. See Rudolf Steiner, *Study of Man: General Education Course*, Stuttgart, August–September 1919, Rudolf Steiner Press, London, 1966. See also *The Younger Generation: Educational and Spiritual Impulses for Life in the Twentieth Century*, Stuttgart, October 1922, Anthroposophic Press, New York, 1984.

12   Hippocrates of Cos, 460–377 BC. Greek physician, founder of ancient medicine.

13   Emperor Frederick III, 1831–88. Suffered from a disease of the larynx. It is not known who wrote the request.

14   Nicholas Copernicus, 1473–1543. Astronomer.

15   Arthur Schopenhauer, 1788–1860. Philosopher.

16   Venus' fly-trap (*Dionaea muscipula*), found in swamps in the warmer part of North America. See Charles Darwin, *Insectivorous Plants*, 1875.

17   Hermann Rollett, 1819–1904. Austrian writer. See Rudolf Steiner, *The Younger Generation* (mentioned above), page 150.

18   In the previous edition of this book, editor Stephen E. Usher presented the following commentary in his Introduction: 'In the light of the fact that an object weighing over 200 lbs landed on Mars and sent back pictures by means of equipment that has proved effective in similar situations and that these pictures show Mars to be a rocky desert, the above statement by Rudolf Steiner can only be judged inaccurate. But the matter is far more complex than the simple juxtaposition of these two statements suggests.

      To form any judgment about these two statements we must have some sense of how Steiner reached his conclusion. We know that he was able to enter higher states of consciousness that he termed Imagination, Inspiration and Intuition. In the state of Imagination the human soul moves within a realm that can be compared with a two-dimensional space of colour images. In true Imagination, consciousness does not experience itself as observing these images from outside the two-dimensional realm but instead as spread out over this two-dimensional realm and interwoven with all the images. Before even elementary observations can be made with accuracy, the soul must develop considerable self-knowledge so as not to confuse itself with objective Imaginations.

The development of Inspiration and Intuition then allows one to interpret what is experienced. Even after these states have been achieved, it is a considerable task to direct one's gaze toward specific Imaginations. In particular, Steiner makes clear that it is possible to find within the Imaginative world the inner realities that relate to specific outer events in space and time. However, the quality of the Imaginative world is movement. Space and time are both derived from movement as was already known to Aristotle.

Finding one's way in Imagination to a specific time in relation to a specific spatial reality — for example Mars at the time of the lecture — may have been particularly difficult. The description Steiner gives of Mars is quite consistent with his general picture of the evolution of the cosmos; it appears to be more characteristic of an earlier planetary condition. Readers familiar with his evolutionary picture will know that he views world evolution as a gradual condensation of solid forms out of originally much softer forms. In earlier ages a more watery condition was the densest condition obtained by matter. Still earlier worlds achieved only the state of air or gas. And most problematic for materialistic thinkers is the idea that the first material condition, which is preceded by purely soul and spiritual ones, is that of pure warmth, radiant heat.

It is possible that Steiner did make a mistake in his location of the actual time in his description of Mars as it appears in this volume. Another possibility is that he was unable to adequately translate the living images of the Imaginative world into conceptual form in this particular case. Incidentally, the reader should be aware that this translation is by no means an easy task and that Steiner is the first occultist to accomplish this work on a vast scale.

A third possibility was suggested by Dr Unger in a lecture delivered in Spring Valley in 1985: that Steiner did not even want to fully translate the imaginative picture because he might have wished to give his listeners an old though still spiritually valid picture. He might have done this to insulate the souls of the workmen from the deadening influence that materialism works on the soul in the life after death. In considering this possibility one should realize that only the workmen were allowed to attend these lectures.

A final consideration which could account for the discrepancy between Steiner's statement and the one resulting from the recent space mission is that there is after all a time difference between these two events of some 60 years. Though most people would find it far-fetched, it is possible that Mars actually went through a considerable condensation over that period. On this point Dr Unger, in the same lecture, observed that the intensity of materialistic thinking in our time is a force leading to such densification of the cosmos.

While the above thoughts do not offer a clear resolution of the discrepancy, they do point to the complexity of the issue, and they also should make clear that even if Steiner was not completely accurate on this point, it does not constitute a challenge to the totality of his work, that has born fruit in many practical fields such as the Waldorf schools, biodynamic agriculture and anthroposophical medicine, to mention a few. These practical applications were all the result of his spiritual research, and their wide success and acceptance lends support to the validity of the underlying method out of which they arose.'

19   See Rudolf Steiner, *Occult History*, Rudolf Steiner Press, London, 1982. Lecture V: '... so-called canals on Mars. There it is a matter of certain streams of force which correspond to an earlier stage of the earth...'

20   At Koberwitz, 7–16 June 1924. See Rudolf Steiner, *Agriculture*, Rudolf Steiner Press, London, 1974.

21   This lecture was postponed to Saturday 13 September.

22   The 'synodic' revolution, that is, the time between two successive conjunctions or oppositions to the sun, varies with Mars between 2 years 34 days and 2 years 80 days, the average time therefore being 2 years 50 days.

23   Matthias Jakob Schleiden, 1804–81, naturalist. Gustav Theodor Fechner, 1801–87, naturalist; founder of psychophysics. See his publication *Professor Schleiden und der Mond*, Leipzig 1856.

24   There is a period of 243 years 2 days in which the intervals between the Venus transits are 8 years, $121\frac{1}{2}$ years, 8 years and $105\frac{1}{2}$ years. The last transit took place on 6 December 1882. According to astronomical calculation the next transit will be on 7 June 2004.

25   The Waldorf School, Stuttgart, Germany, opened in 1919 under Rudolf Steiner's guidance. There are now more than 300 schools in the international Waldorf School movement.

26   This lecture was postponed to Thursday 18 September.

27   Ferdinand Hochstetter, 1829–84. Geographer and geologist.

28   Active volcano in Mexico.

29   Ernst Haeckel, 1834–1919. Biologist and philosopher.

30   The so-called 'little Weigel house', built in 1647, demolished in 1898 when Weigelstrasse was constructed. One of the 'Seven Wonders of Jena'. It was seven stories high and contained a circular staircase through which one could look up by day and see the stars shining in the heavens.

31   Rudolf Falb, 1838–1903. See *Grundzüge der Theorie der Erdbeben und Vulkanausbrüche*, Graz 1870; *Gedanken und Studien über den Vulkanismus*, Graz 1875.

32   Goethe vehemently opposed the ideas on volcanoes held by Leopold von Buch and others, which were at that time becoming well known, and which in his opinion lacked a central idea that could have illumined the individual facts. See his letter to Nees von Esenbeck, 13 June 1823.

33   Julius Robert Mayer, 1814–78. See *Beiträge zur Dynamik des Himmels*, Heilbronn, 1848.

34   Karl von Nagler, 1770–1846, Prussian statesman. Postmaster 1823–46. Initiated our modern mail system.

35   See R. Hagen, *Die erste deutsche Eisenbahn*, 1885.

36   Sir Francis Drake, 1540–96. Famous British navigator.

37   J.J.L. Lalande, 1732–1807. French astronomer.

38   Joseph Johann Littrow, 1781–1840, *Über den gefürchteten Kometen des Jahres 1832 und über Kometen überhaupt*, 1832.

39   Wolfram von Eschenbach, 1170–1220, *Parsival*, completed in 1210. Richard Wagner, 1813–83, *Parsifal*, 'a sacred dramatic festival' appeared as a poem in 1877; the opera was finished in 1882.

40   Rudolf Steiner taught in the Arbeiterbildungschule, a workmen's college in Berlin during 1899 to 1904. See *Autobiography*, chap. 28, Anthroposophic Press, New York, 1999.

41   Ferdinand Lassalle, 1825–64. Founder of Socialism in Germany.

42   This scheduled lecture did not take place. The lecture of 24 September 1924 that concluded this volume was the last Rudolf Steiner was able to give to the workmen. The illness which led to his death began a few days later.

Note Regarding Rudolf Steiner's Lectures

The lectures and addresses contained in this volume have been translated from the German, which is based on stenographic and other recorded texts that were in most cases never seen or revised by the lecturer. Hence, due to human errors in hearing and transcription, they may contain mistakes and faulty passages. Every effort has been made to ensure that this is not the case. Some of the lectures were given to audiences more familiar with anthroposophy; these are the so-called 'private' or 'members' lectures. Other lectures, like the written works, were intended for the general public. The difference between these, as Rudolf Steiner indicates in his *Autobiography*, is twofold. On the one hand, the members' lectures take for granted a background in and commitment to anthroposophy; in the public lectures this was not the case. At the same time, the members' lectures address the concerns and dilemmas of the members, while the public work speaks directly out of Steiner's own understanding of universal needs. Nevertheless, as Rudolf Steiner stresses: 'Nothing was ever said that was not solely the result of my direct experience of the growing content of anthroposophy. There was never any question of concessions to the prejudices and preferences of the members. Whoever reads these privately printed lectures can take them to represent anthroposophy in the fullest sense. Thus it was possible without hesitation—when the complaints in this direction became too persistent—to depart from the custom of circulating this material "For members only". But it must be borne in mind that faulty passages do occur in these reports not revised by myself.' Earlier in the same chapter, he states: 'Had I been able to correct them [the private lectures], the restriction *for members only* would have been unnecessary from the beginning.'

The original German editions on which this text is based were published by Rudolf Steiner Verlag, Dornach, Switzerland in the collected edition (*Gesamtausgabe*, 'GA') of Rudolf Steiner's work. All publications are edited by the Rudolf Steiner Nachlassverwaltung (estate), which wholly owns both Rudolf Steiner Verlag and the Rudolf Steiner Archive. The organization relies solely on donations to continue its activity.

For further information please contact:

Rudolf Steiner Archiv
Postfach 135
CH-4143 Dornach

or:

www.rudolf-steiner.com

Rudolf Steiner
FROM CRYSTALS TO CROCODILES...
Answers to Questions

Speech and languages; lefthandedness; dinosaurs; Lemuria; turtles and crocodiles; oxygen and carbon; ancient giant oysters; the moon, sun and earth; the Old Testament; the real nature of Adam; breathing and brain activity; dreams; sugar; the liver and perception; brain cells and thinking; cancer and its origin; diabetes; the eyes of animals; Paracelsus; alcohol, and migraine.

ISBN 1 85584 107 X; £11.95; 192pp

Rudolf Steiner
FROM MAMMOTHS TO MEDIUMS...
Answers to Questions

Dancing and sport; guardian angels; effects of the stars; potatoes, beetroot and radishes; the Druids; Roman Catholic and Masonic rituals; proteins, fats, carbohydrates and salts; Aristotle; nutrition; blood circulation and the heart; honesty and conscience; boredom and opinions; lungs and kidneys; fertilization in plants and humans; light and colour; and breathing.

ISBN 1 85584 078 2; £14.95; 328pp

Rudolf Steiner
FROM COMETS TO COCAINE...
Answers to Questions

Nicotine and alcohol; the causes and timing of illness; pregnancy; vegetarian and meat diets; the human ear, eye and hair colour; influenza, hay fever, haemophilia; planets and metals; mental illness; the ice age; the thyroid gland and hormones; beavers, wasps and bees; the nose, smell and taste; and jaundice, smallpox and rabies.

ISBN 1 85584 088 X; £14.95; 320pp

Rudolf Steiner
FROM ELEPHANTS TO EINSTEIN...
Answers to Questions

Ants and bees; shells and skeletons; animal and plant poisons—arsenic and lead; nutrition—protein and fats, potatoes; the human eye and its colour; fresh and salt water; fish and bird migration; human clothing; opium and alcohol; thinking, and bodily secretions.

ISBN 1 85584 081 2; £10.95; 208pp